A Maze of Grace

Also by Trish Ryan:

He Loves Me, He Loves Me Not:
A Memoir of Finding Faith, Hope, and Happily Ever After

A Maze of Grace

A MEMOIR OF SECOND CHANCES

Trish Ryan

NEW YORK   BOSTON   NASHVILLE

FaithWords
Hachette Book Group
237 Park Avenue
New York, NY 10017

www.faithwords.com

Printed in the United States of America

First Edition: June 2010
10 9 8 7 6 5 4 3 2 1

FaithWords is a division of Hachette Book Group, Inc.
The FaithWords name and logo are trademarks of Hachette Book Group, Inc.

Library of Congress Cataloging-in-Publication Data
Ryan, Trish.
A maze of grace : a memoir of second chances / Trish Ryan. — 1st ed.
    p. cm.
ISBN 978-0-446-54581-5
1. Wives — Religious life.   2. Christian women — Religious life.
3. Marriage — Religious aspects — Christianity.   4. Ryan, Trish.   I. Title.
BV4528.15.R93 2010
248.8'435 — dc22
                                                                    2009052850

For Steve—
Here's to happily ever after, and green.

The Requisite Memoir Disclaimer

NAMES HAVE BEEN CHANGED to protect the innocent. Time sequences have been somewhat altered because real life unfolds with a frustrating disregard for literary narrative structure. I refer to God as a man and I hope that won't keep you from reading this if you have a more gender-neutral viewpoint. And finally, as with my first book, there's some colorful language. Not as much as I had in the first draft, certainly, but enough to convey that I'm still not the kind of girl who yells "Oh sugar!" when I stub my toe.

Contents

Introduction   *xiii*

1. The Meaning of Wife   1
2. A Wrinkle in Time   12
3. That's Just Swell   19
4. Give That Man Some Sex   30
5. Little Foxes   42
6. Seeds   61
7. The Trouble with Multiplication   76
8. The Secret   87
9. Getting a Sleigh to Fly   101
10. Cocktail Parties   114
11. Seek   126
12. You're Still Pro-Choice, Right?   137
13. Settle?   153
14. Glimpses of Grace   165
15. One More Girl Who Got Stuffed in Some Jeans   179
16. Covered   194
17. Story   204
18. Heroes, Hope, and Rescue   213
19. Four Words   222

Acknowledgments   *227*

For this is one of the miracles of love; it gives — to both, but perhaps especially to the woman — a power of seeing through its own enchantments and yet not being disenchanted.

— C.S. Lewis

Introduction

WE WERE JUST A few months shy of our fifth anniversary the first time Steve lied to me. It wasn't a big lie. It wouldn't even register with most couples as meriting a conversation. But for me it was crushing, a small betrayal threatening to take down the walls of trust we'd built and eat us both alive. It was as if all of a sudden a snake had appeared in our living room and was now writhing around between us, and all we could do was look at each other and wonder what the hell happened and how we were supposed to deal with it.

We were, to put it mildly, stressed. Steve had just accepted a new job, we were moving, our condo wasn't selling, and we were stuck in an awful sort of limbo that helped us understand our Catholic ancestors' concept of purgatory. He'd been home sick all day, took two NyQuil tablets, and was zonked. As I tucked him in that night, he said, "I need to tell you something..."

It wasn't such a big thing. The thing itself barely mattered. But Steve — *my* Steve, the guy who'd taught me how to love like I'd never been hurt before — had lied to me. I didn't have space for that in my brain. I sat on the edge of the bed staring blankly at the wall, gasping — discreetly, I hoped; for some reason I felt like I had to keep up a facade of cool—for air.

"I'm so sorry," he said.

"I forgive you," I said. This was our practice—to ask forgiveness, and forgive. First, before we talked things out. It was our desperate way of inviting God into impossible situations. We knew He'd tell us to forgive each other eventually, and that forgiveness carried tangible spiritual power. So we'd get it out there in the beginning, in the hopes that it would help us navigate the bumps to come. I didn't have much faith in that power that night, though. I wasn't certain what forgiveness meant. "This makes me wonder," I said, "what else haven't you told me?" *Here is where it starts*, I thought, bracing myself for the worst as a wave of hopelessness crashed through me. Steve looked at me blankly, like he didn't understand the question. Then the NyQuil kicked in. I watched, befuddled, as my contrite husband disappeared behind a curtain of five-syllable ingredients designed to give him a good night's rest. Three minutes later, he was sound asleep, and I was alone with the snake.

I wandered out into the kitchen in an angry, quiet daze. I was tired but I didn't want to go to bed. Not that bed, not with him. I could sleep on the couch, I thought. But that seemed out of proportion to the offense. I spent the next two hours sipping Cabernet and watching a reality show about a family with eighteen children. After that I did that awful nighttime thing you do when you're hurt and scared and mad: I skulked through the dark into our room, slipped in on my side, and clung to the edge of the bed like there were demons in the middle. I was fiercely, irrationally determined not to touch him, wake him, or acknowledge his presence in any way. Then I lay there for another hour wondering what to do.

It had been a long time since I'd felt this way. Almost five years, to be exact. Before Steve, I'd spent fifteen years in the dating trenches. I'd been married once before, and I'd been lied to plenty. So I came into our relationship with an entire arsenal of professional-grade scorned-woman tactics up my sleeve that I could reach for at any time. I hadn't needed them, which was good, because scorned-woman tactics tend to blow things up rather than pull them back together. But what else could I do? Pretend it never happened? I'd seen others try that, and fail (we women aren't nearly as good at hiding our fury as we think). I ran scenarios through my mind, trying to decide how to deal with this betrayal. "I should give him the silent treatment in the morning and ignore him all day so he'll know how upset I am," I thought.

That's when I heard the Voice. It was soothing, but firm. It sounded like God. *Wait*—He said. *Do you really want to set up a situation where Steve dreads coming home?*

"Well then we could have a long talk tomorrow night over dinner about the damage this does to my confidence— relationally, sexually..."

Are you sure you want him to see you as sexually pathetic and unapproachable? That seems like it will cost more than you'll gain.

"Well, I should at least wake him up and insist that we talk about this now...all the experts say not to go to bed angry..." I was grasping for straws at this point, quasi-quoting magazine articles I couldn't quite remember to justify shaking Steve awake so I could make him feel as sad and scared as I did.

That's ridiculous, God said. *You know Steve feels horrible about this. You know he'd be awake if he weren't drugged. And you know he'll do anything in his power to make this up to you tomorrow. Don't force a fight that's bigger than this just because you're feeling neglected.*

We went on like this, God and I, for about an hour. Finally, I ran out of snappy ideas.

Then He said (wisely, gently, firmly): *It does no good to cry, yell, or ignore a man who is passed out on pharmaceuticals. Get some sleep.*

Afterwards, I felt an odd calm, like some grandmotherly angel flew by and wrapped me in a blanket.

The next morning, Steve and I didn't immediately snap back to being "us," but we were closer than I expected. The snake seemed smaller. We killed it together, then took it out to the dumpster. We cleaned up the rug (Note for literalists: This is a METAPHOR. You won't find snake bits if you go through our garbage; there's no need to alert PETA) and got on with our lives.

✦

One of the best parts of my faith is that it allows do-overs. Jesus is the only spiritual leader I've found who says, *Come to me when you've messed up and I'll give you a second chance.* This book is a collection of the ways I've taken him up on this offer. My history is littered with stories of me jumping wildly into one pool or another, never once thinking to check whether or not it held any water. I've gotten better, just as Jesus suggested I would. But growing up rarely happens in a straight trajectory. More often it comes in wild surges and sudden U-turns, and that's been the case with me. Steve and I wandered around corners and up over hills expecting to find Happily Ever After, only to be blindsided by things we never saw coming. And yet we were also blindsided—or blanketed, depending on your perspective—by grace we never anticipated, and a God who has taken infinitely good care of us each awkward step of the way.

My friend Will says that happiness is when life exceeds your expectations. By that standard, we're in pretty good shape. It turns out I wasn't crazy, clinging to my romantic view of marriage for all those years like Kate Winslet clutching that floating door at the end of *Titanic*. I'm more convinced than ever that this mysterious, elusive state—where life exceeds our expectations on a regular, surprising basis—is real, that we can get there. But I wonder if it isn't like the city of Avalon lurking in the mist, or Platform Nine and Three-quarters in *Harry Potter*—if you have to believe it exists before you can see it? Sometimes, it's hard to believe. But just because something is hard doesn't mean it's not worth the effort.

Lately, I've been thinking about two quotes: one by the Apostle Peter, the other from Virginia Woolf. At some level, they're irreconcilable. And yet they've been cohabitating in my mind for months now, jockeying for my allegiance. The first, from Peter, says, "Always be prepared to give an answer to everyone who asks you to give the reason for the hope that you have." That seems easy enough. But then Virginia Woolf suggests that I lower my expectations for what my "answer" can accomplish: "When a subject is highly controversial—and any question about sex is that," she warns, "one cannot hope to tell the truth. One can only show how one came to hold whatever opinion one does hold."

This is my goal. I've worked the parameters of relationships and happily ever after more than any other question in life. I have some opinions on the subject. I know the reason for the hope that I have. But I can think of at least sixteen people who will throw this book across the room in frustrated horror when they read how this worked for me so far. Oh well. Maybe, in a moment of hope or desperation (or routine spring cleaning) they'll pick the book back up again and wonder how things played out. (If that's you, welcome back.)

⁂

"You *should* write about your life now," my friend Kristen insisted. We were on the phone on a Saturday afternoon, and I was confessing my struggles to come up with a viable proposal for a new book. I wasn't sure that these new experiences, delightful and complex though they were, warranted multiple chapters of examination.

"How can you say that?" I asked. "Every time you call and ask how I'm doing, all I ever say is, 'Great!' I can't even explain why it's great; we both know it's not because of me. It's just sort of this crazy miracle. Why would anyone want to read about that?"

"Because," she said softly, "until you and I started having these conversations, I never knew life could work out that way. Maybe there are a bunch of us out here who need to know that it can."

That's why I'm writing this book. It is, I guess, what I was looking for when I was in Kristen's shoes, newly raw from a marital breakdown, defensive, hurt, fighting off hopelessness. I needed encouragement that something other than what I'd experienced was possible. I didn't need any more warnings; I needed a lifeline, and a way to sort things out. I needed to know that, in the event my prayers for a husband were answered, God would also hear my prayers for our marriage, and for the rest of my life. He did, and He does, and if it encourages you at all to know the story, then you have Kristen to thank.

A brief disclaimer: I'm under no illusion that Steve and I have mastered some spiritual "right" way to do life. But as we've given God room to work in our lives, asking for His input in places we were stuck, He's given us ideas and solutions and alternative routes around roadblocks that have changed our experience. The Bible says that God will help anyone who asks, so that's the extent of my advice: ask. The rest is just our story.

And our story, like that of every marriage, includes more than the two of us bumping into one another and figuring things out. We've been through some ups and downs: navigating personal struggles (infertility, depression), universal questions (body image, what makes good sex?), and humbling moments (awkward conversations, leaning harder than expected on our family and friends). We're still on the front end of figuring out what it means to use the Bible as the road map for our lives: both the existential "Why are we here?" questions about meaning and purpose and destiny, and the practical "Why are we here?" questions about living in a huge, secular city where there's garbage on the streets, a housing project two doors down, and the mortgage on our one-bedroom condo would afford us a mansion anywhere else in the country. The challenge of our new life, as it turns out, has been only partly about figuring out how to relate to each other. Instead, the bulk of our efforts have gone toward our struggle to discern (if you'll forgive the obnoxious, navel-gazing sound of this) how we fit in with the rest of the world. This is why I ended my first book at our wedding. Narratively speaking, it made sense to pause for a moment and ponder the incredible fact that God came through on His promise to bring me a husband if I'd take Jesus seriously. But this was also a convenient stopping place, because as I wrote the scenes from our courtship and wedding day, Steve and I were in the throes of questioning (and being questioned about) every facet of our newly minted happily ever after. Along with the usual considerations regarding the allocation of household chores and whether or not we actually *liked* sex on the beach now that we were free to try it—and I'm not talking about the drink—we found ourselves in the middle of the larger conversation of who and what we were about. The time had come, in the words of the Apostle Paul, "to work out our salvation."

One of my favorite songs promises that if I follow God, He'll lead me through a maze of grace. So far, that's been true. The path has taken some wild twists and turns, with forks requiring instant decisions coming up about every half mile. It sometimes feels like that Robert Frost poem "The Road Not Taken," as I wonder how to make choices I'll be glad for later, rather than ones I'll regret. But when I look up, when I pause to ask, God is right there.

I think God promises two things to help us through the maze: encouragement and information. That's what this book is about. I want to encourage you that there's grace in the maze, that God cares about us—individually, personally—and how our lives go. In a way, tapping into this grace is like accessing a divine GPS system: it might take some effort to recalibrate, but the results are worth it. As Kristen requested, this book is kind of like aerial surveillance, zooming in on different views of what life has been like during these first few years: funny, loving, poignant, sad, furious, brilliant, humbling... But the best word for these years is *encouraging*. I'm encouraged that marriage can be so much better than I'd dared imagine. I'm encouraged that Jesus has answers when I don't. I'm encouraged that prayer works, that God loves love, and that the heart-catching words in Ecclesiastes about how "a cord of three strands is not easily broken" are so very true when we lean into them. My hope with these stories is to pass this along, to fill the void in writing about spirituality and relationships and say: *be encouraged.*

A Maze of Grace

Chapter 1

The Meaning of Wife

WHEN STEVE AND I walked back down the aisle after our pastor Brian pronounced us man and wife, my head wasn't filled with airy-fairy notions of how we'd cuddle all day and make love all night (although I hoped there'd be a fair amount of both). My vision of happily ever after was less about candlelight dinners and rolling around in rose petals, and more about buying potholders and ordering checks with our names listed together in the upper left-hand corner. I was *excited* to share the mundane tasks of life: burnt meatloaf, clogged sinks in the bathroom, a dog chewing happily on the upholstery of a brand new couch. To me, this was the good stuff. It wasn't about money, or even decorating, per se; it was about Steve and me together in the same kitchen, our names together on the same checks. It was about bills that were *ours*, for trips or furniture or electricity we'd gone on or purchased or used up together — you know, in *our house*, because we were married, and that's what married people do: married people build a life together, making choices about how to invest their time and effort and money and attention, dreaming of something bigger than either one of them can pull off on their own. I was excited to finally be part of that.

I'd spent my twenties and half of my thirties crying over one breakup after another, and scheduling my life around episodes of *Mad About You*, a sitcom about an unremarkable newlywed couple and their unremarkable life. To me, lonely, scared and single, the security Paul and Jamie Buchman shared in their New York City apartment was remarkable. I wanted a photo montage like the one that rolled in the opening credits of that sitcom, snapshots of Steve and me doing normal things — reading the paper, sharing an ice cream cone, running hand in hand to catch the train — together. Not because we'd made special plans, but because our everyday lives were intertwined. After being alone for so long, wondering if it would always be that way — if any man would ever care with me about my meatloaf, my clogged sink, my new puppy — it was nothing short of divine to find myself in the midst of real domestic bliss, to have outward evidence of this inward covenant where God somehow made us one.

The night before my wedding, my sister, Meg, and my best friend, Kristen, had taken me out for dinner and drinks. After placing a blinking bridal tiara on my head, they gave me a gag gift, a book called *Mrs. Dunwoody's Excellent Instructions for Homekeeping*. They'd meant it as a joke, but in the early days of my new marriage I pored over its pages like it held the secret to some hidden kingdom. It was late June, and I was uncharacteristically sad to have missed out on spring cleaning. I cast about our small condo for something to whitewash. As strange as it sounds, I loved the mundane aspects of wifedom: doing our laundry, seeing my jeans next to Steve's boxers, his giant Timberland T-shirts mixed in with mine from Ann Taylor. If I was doing my husband's laundry, that meant I had *a husband*. For me, that was the whole point.

"What do you mean, you do Steve's laundry?" Rina asked me, eyes wide with horror.

"You're not working? Not at all?" Caryn looked at me like I'd just hopped off of the set of *Little House on the Prairie*.

"You took Steve's name?" Marcia demanded. "You're not even going to hyphenate?" She was dangerously close to hyperventilating.

"She's new at this," they reassured each other, as if I wasn't right there in the room. "The honeymoon will be over soon; then she'll know the truth."

"Marriage is hard," said Rina.

"Marriage is hard," Caryn admitted.

"Marriage is *hard*," Marcia insisted, defying me to disagree. It was like they were envoys from the Island of Wife, sent to initiate me into their grim sorority of disappointed princesses, tamping down my enthusiasm lest I become overly optimistic about my new status. *It's a tough job*, their faces said, *but somebody has to do it.*

I tried to fend them off, to protect myself from the bitter hexes they tossed out. I asked them, over and over, *Do you remember what it was like to be single?* For me, the lonely nights and life questions faced alone—that set the bar for "hard." It seems they had forgotten.

This clash of worldviews proved to be a bit of a theme. There I'd be, talking innocently of our efforts to build a fun life (assuming that the women around me were chasing that same dream), only to be met with silence, scorn, and the occasional furrowed brow. I didn't yet know that my audacity ran headlong into the societal conviction that if I was anywhere near as happy as I appeared to be, then clearly I didn't know a thing about marriage. There seemed to be some unwritten rule that until you'd been married long enough to recognize how *hard* this institution was, your experience was nothing more than an ephemeral, Disney-esque utopia, utterly distinct from couples doing time in the real trenches of wedded bliss, people who knew that marriage was work, conflict, compromise, and struggle. You know, *hard*.

A newlywed friend told me about attending a bridal shower for her cousin, how all the women (fortified with a glass or three of truth-serum Chardonnay) had offered up advice about wifehood. "What were the topics?" I asked curiously.

"The usual," my friend said. "You know—how men want more sex than we could ever possibly give them; how once you get married you can kiss your free time goodbye; how no one prepares you for all the sacrifices or tells you what to do when your perfect new husband makes you so angry you want to stab yourself in the eye with a fork."

Oh. *That.*

We talked about how the magical part of so many marriages seems to end when a couple walks off into the sunset to the waning notes of some Elvis ballad; as if somewhere along the line, everyone reached an unspoken agreement that marriage is a bad deal for all involved. Now, it's the brass ring women chase, the slipknot noose men dodge and evade, the shackled inevitability couples settle into once they run out of other things to try. "It's like we've banished marriage to the land of death and taxes," she said, "just one more unavoidable, unpleasant fact of life."

I waited for the other shoe to drop, the one that might prompt me to trash my carefully prepared thoughts on the goodness of living with Steve 'til death do us part. And yet at the same time I prayed (fervently) that it never, ever would.

How does one learn to be a wife these days? I knew what I wanted my marriage to *feel* like, but had no idea what to do to make that happen, how to get there. I had role models, certainly: my mother, my sister, Meg, my friend Pascha. I could have asked them anything. But I didn't. I guess I was afraid of what I'd find out. I had a vision of each of their marriages— happy, intact—that I didn't want to sacrifice. In the wake of so much evidence that marriages fail, I needed these glimmers of hope that marriages succeed.

Looking beyond my immediate circle, I hunkered down to consider all manner of expert advice, absorbing and synthesizing polemics from every side of the debate. I read left-wing feminists, right-wing Christians, recalcitrant activists from the 1960s admitting that they liked staying home to raise their children, and sheepish career women from the 1990s admitting that they'd lose their minds if they were cooped up with their kids all day. I read about women who loved their husbands but didn't like them, women who had sex with their husbands but rarely talked to them, women who worshiped their husbands but were afraid of them, and unmarried women who clung to all manner of vague commitments hoping against hope they'd someday end up in one of the aforementioned categories. All in all, I found, much of marital literature focuses on failure. Happy people are apparently too polite to write books about how well things are going. Perhaps they should. Because what I realized after all that reading was that I'd absorbed some bad (well-intentioned, perhaps, but nonetheless *bad*) advice over the years: *Communication is the most important thing. Sex matters less and less once you're married. Get in touch with your feelings—they'll never lie.* Pardon my candor, but what utter crap. It took Steve and me approximately three days to realize that talking endlessly about our disagreements didn't solve them, sex mattered way more than we'd thought, and my feelings lied all the time about what was really going on. These discoveries left me at the end of myself, with no idea how to make good on this love/honor/cherish agreement we'd made. My intentions were excellent, but I needed a better skill set to back them up.

I reread Anne Morrow Lindbergh's classic book *Gift from the Sea*. It had landed on my shelf years before, a present for my law school graduation. Its pages held a bookmark with the sage reminder that God never closes a door without opening a window (who would have guessed back then just how much opening and closing was to come?). I'd tossed the book aside as I surged out into my life like a modern-day Mary Tyler Moore. But now, as I unpacked my boxes in what had been Steve's bachelor pad, I wondered if her words might have something to say to me; if, from this newly acquired perch of *wife*, I might finally understand.

I sped through the chapters, devouring her lovely prose. The mother of five, Lindbergh was ahead of her time in recognizing that balance and creative mental space can be hard to come by when your world is filled with the demands of tiny human creatures looking to you for guidance, solace, and a peanut butter sandwich (without crust) every day at noon. Her points were beautifully made, yet I couldn't fend off the growing sense that simplicity and some extra vacation time still weren't what I needed. I was at a different end of the life spectrum: until recently, the only demands I'd wrestled with were the ones in my own head, the churning vat of fear and worry that no one would ever look to me expecting... well, anything. Lindbergh longed for time alone, for space to sort out her thoughts. I'd had nothing but aloneness for several years and was well over the illusion that *I* was the answer I was looking for.

It made me wonder, though: what sort of encouragement *did* I need? Were there words of hope out there for these early years of marriage—pearls of wisdom for those of us who don't need more space, but rather long to realize God's promise of supernatural oneness with our new spouse? There's not much, I soon discovered, in terms of helpful guides for building a new marriage. There are lots of repair manuals, and even prescriptions for a complete overhaul when it seems like hope is lost. But what about when hope is found?

❧

Once, I was invited by Ann Taylor to come to their corporate headquarters in New York City to be part of a team of customers offering our opinions on the new fall line. I earned this spot, I suspect, with my AT credit card, and the months and months of retail therapy I'd undergone in the AT dressing room, fending off my lawyerly angst with cute triacetate suits and trendy accessories. There were dozens of us, gathered from all over the country—an assortment of ages, sizes, shapes, and colors—excited for a fun weekend in the city and the chance to talk about clothes. We were paired together and asked to try on different outfits they'd arranged. My partner was Sun-Yi, a tall, willowy investment analyst. Standing together in front of the mirror, we looked like Bert and Ernie.

The first ensemble was a wool suit—loden green, with hints of navy and gold—paired with a wheat-toned sweater shell. It was gorgeous, and as I carried it into the dressing room, I'd already purchased it in my mind and paired it with a cute bag I'd seen at Macy's the week before. A few minutes later, Sun-Yi emerged from her dressing room looking like a model dashing off to a photo shoot. I came out of my room looking like Princess Fiona from Shrek.

On me, the suit was ghastly. The green sapped every hint of rose from my complexion, rendering me translucent and vaguely purple. The pants narrowed so severely from hip to ankle that it looked as if I'd been pruned; I resembled nothing so much as an inverted evergreen. And the wool itched. Sun-Yi stood serenely while answering questions about fit and use from the Ann Taylor team; I twitched and squirmed and struggled not to rip the fabric from my body. I felt—as I have so many times—like a short, fat failure. Who was I to think I could look good next to the tall, thin Sun-Yi's of the world, women with the genetic good fortune to measure the same at hip and ankle, whose complexion didn't ebb and flow in response to variations in room temperature, fabric choice, or embarrassment?

When the Ann Taylor executives had completed their pictures and seventeen-point analysis, we were freed to try on the next outfit. I sprinted off, peeling the jacket from my hive-covered arms as I went. I wrestled my way into the next ensemble. We had jeans this time, and mine slid on with surprising ease, hugging my curves and buttoning at the perfect place. They were paired with an assortment of colorful cashmere sweaters; we'd been instructed to start with blue. I was first out of the dressing room, and relieved by what I saw. I looked cute, like a young professional dashing out on a Saturday afternoon to buy brie and crackers for a cocktail party. Sun-Yi came out and I gasped: She looked terrible. The jeans bagged pitifully from every dimension of her hips and backside, and the blue sweater—which looked rich and jewel-toned on me—made her look like an Easter egg.

This was a revelation. It suggested the audacious possibility that just because something didn't work for me didn't mean it was inherently awful, it was simply not for me. My perfect fit might be another woman's nightmare, and vice versa.

I thought back on this time now, and how it had broader implications than just shopping. What if I quit squishing myself into ill-fitting loden green suits? What if I held out for the curvy jeans and flattering sweater, rather than spending my life resigned to being itchy and pale? What if I kept looking until I found something—clothing, a way to live, an approach to wife and life—that fit?

⌘

I once worked with a guy who had a giant wall of bookshelves in his apartment. As a book lover, I was entranced by his collection of titles. "Where did you get all these?" I asked.

"They're from IKEA," he said, thinking I meant the shelves. "Whenever I'm dating a girl and it seems like things might get serious, I buy one of these for us to put together. They're close to impossible—directions in every language but English, an assortment of extra pieces you don't need—I figure that if I meet a woman and we can do this together without killing each other, she *must* be the one for me."

I counted seventeen shelves stacked up against his wall. "Wow," I said. "You must be a complete jerk."

I thought of John and his IKEA system at various times over that first year. I think he was onto something with his ideas about what it takes to build a solid relationship, but he introduced the test too early. I'm not sure how Steve and I would have fared on a project of this complexity. But after we said our vows and embarked upon our new life together, I realized that John was right—marriage *is* like building a bookshelf from IKEA: complicated, but doable. We had to lay out all the pieces we'd been given: expectations from how we were raised, previous relationships, things we'd seen or read or heard; hopes we'd created in our minds as we dreamt about this moment; tangible requirements of life such as jobs that needed attention, families that needed love, friendships that would either adapt or fade away. And the ancient legacies we carried with us: the demands of feminism, the suggestions of the religious right, left, and center; the millions upon millions of pages written to offer contradictory advice as to the essence of a good marriage (as if one size could ever fit all). When we arrived home from our honeymoon, unpacked our gifts, and spread out all the pieces we had to build with, we had far more than we could possibly use. Choices had to be made about what would stay and what would go, and we needed guidance to help us make those decisions. Steve and I could do this deliberately, we soon discovered, making decisions together about how we hoped this all would work (and risk annoying friends who couldn't believe I was already washing my husband's laundry) or we could try to build around the extra flotsam we had no use for until it crowded us into a corner. This was our work in those first months — sorting through the pieces, deciding what to keep, what would help us thrive, and what sort of structure our life would take. We still had more questions than answers, and felt rather precarious winging it as we cast about for the shape of our new lives.

Chapter 2

A Wrinkle in Time

THAT'S WHEN I DISCOVERED Madeleine L'Engle. She's
not usually heralded as a self-help author, but rather as the genius crafter of magical childhood tales. Her children's stories
led me to her memoirs: four volumes chronicling her life as a
writer, woman, and wife. She was wise, in the way you want a
mentor to be. What's most notable, though, is how utterly true
her words were for me, even though they were written four decades earlier. She wrote about how she and her husband—two
people as different as the day is long—were sustained for forty
years by the promises they made when they wed, and that even
though they were young and naïve, *a promise is a promise*, so
they hung in there through the fights and the struggles and the
times when one or both might have liked to walk away. They
read the Bible, and believed what it said. Simple stuff, this.

L'Engle talked about the importance of boundaries—not
between her and her husband, but around them. She noted
how little my generation likes this topic. We've been raised,
after all, on the rally-cry of freedom, of rebellion and not wanting

to be fenced in, held back, told what to do. "You're miserable, for the most part," she said, "but you're free. Amoebas are also free, but I don't think they have much fun."

I thought back to the conversation with my friend just back from that bridal shower. I'd certainly seen enough couples go through genuine struggles: bankruptcy, betrayal, sickness where they'd hoped for health. I knew that marriage *could* be hard. I just didn't believe that it had to be, or that underwear left on the bedroom floor or a sink left unrinsed after shaving necessarily made it so. I couldn't forget all the weddings I'd witnessed with pews filled with family and friends wide-eyed with hope and wonder, captivated by tangible awe that two people found each other in our crazy maze of a world. Being *chosen* is a powerful thing. It takes more than just awe, though, to make a union work. This was L'Engle's point about what haunts our generation: We're so enamored of our freedom that we lack the framework on which to build a life. We're like the amoebas—unhindered by skeletons, able to shape-shift into unlimited new and creative forms. But we can't sustain them. We don't have the structure we need to hold our pieces in place once we've lined them up. Her words made me long for such a structure; for a sturdy home built on a rock rather than a quick, fragile sandcastle.

After that, it seemed like everything around me pointed in this same direction. My favorite singer Nichole Nordeman sang about a rocky patch in her own marriage in a song called "We Build." I watched a documentary about Amish crafts-men, and how they put barns up in a single day because they know the importance of getting the roof on. I heard a sermon about Jesus being the cornerstone, and how important it is to select the cornerstone wisely because it sets the entire house. The advice I was looking for in those first months of marriage wasn't, I realized, *Gift from the Sea*, so much as *The Basics of Sound Construction*.

Not many people think of the Bible as a book of spiritual wisdom these days, and hardly anyone believes God's claim that the book is, in fact, *alive*—that the words on those pages will speak to us in specific circumstances like a personalized letter sent to assuage our deepest fears. A recent *Newsweek* article asked, "Would any contemporary heterosexual married couple— who likely woke up on their wedding day harboring some optimistic and newfangled ideas about gender equality and romantic love—turn to the Bible as a how-to script?" Well, yes. Us. Steve and me, following in the steps of L'Engle and her husband and countless others before us, were that contemporary heterosexual married couple who turned to the Bible as our how-to script. Underneath that leather cover, we found a treasure trove of stories and ideas suggesting that divorce statistics weren't destiny, and my worst-case scenario wasn't necessarily the end of the story.

Unlike most books, the Bible doesn't end with the man finding the woman of his dreams and riding off into the sunset. It *starts* there. Adam and Eve frolic in bliss by page three, and are hip deep in a mess they can't clean up by page four. God starts His book with the presumption that if we haven't made a wreck of things yet, we're about to. After that you see devastation, exile, miraculous rescue, and then a long, long journey through the desert, where God takes his people across not one but two raging rivers and into the Promised Land.

But even then, God didn't just hand out nicely manicured half-acre plots to the desert-weary Israelites. They had to fight to take it over. The rest of the Bible can aptly be called, "How To Inhabit the Land." It's a collection of stories of what God told His people to do, the good results when they listened, the disasters when they didn't. And the plan God came up with to save us all from ourselves. Most importantly (to me, at least) it promised that Jesus could do "exceedingly, abundantly above all we can ask or imagine" for people who love Him. That's what I was after. It felt like we'd been invited into an alternate universe, where God was *for* us in a way we didn't usually take into account. When I opened the Bible, it felt like God kept saying, *"Nothing is like you thought it was, but so much more is possible..."*

～✿～

One summer when we were on vacation with my sister and her family, Meg gave me Louise Dickinson Rich's memoir of living deep in the Maine woods in the 1940s. I loved it. In simple, sparse language, Rich offers this brief explanation of what made her marriage work: *they needed each other.* Theirs wasn't a vague, emotionally driven sort of need, although I don't doubt that in a community of only nine people, companionship was a huge benefit of their union. The need she described was real; it had facets she and her husband could point to and say, "If you didn't do that, I'd be in trouble." Either of them could have eked out a survival on their own; most of us can. But to thrive, to have space to reach out and live, they needed each other. "I believe that a great many marriages fail," she said, "because there is no true dependence between the partners... It's a terribly trite thing to say, I know, but most of us have to be needed to be happy."

Until that point, I hadn't realized how hard I'd been fighting the admission that I need Steve, and that I like that he needs me. It seems like such a regressive and pathetic state in this day and age... and yet in real life, this mutual dependence is one of the best things I've ever been part of. I feel like a double agent, caught between the truth (that I need Steve to understand what's going on with our 401(k) plan, remember which week they pick up recycling, and to think to call the furnace man when the weather is still warm to make sure we'll have heat when it isn't), and the societal pressure for me to insist that I can do everything on my own. Can I do these things? Of course. To some extent, in different times and circumstances, I have. But not all that well. And there are things Steve needs me for: I remember plans we've made with people and what time we should be there. I know where lost things can be found, and when the dog needs to go to the vet to make sure she won't get rabies or heartworm or Lyme. I read people and situations (and books and magazines) more quickly than he does, and so usually have a bigger well of information to pull from when evaluating what's going on around us. Together, we're a pretty good team.

It's not cool to need, I've noticed. At least not in a romantic context. I'm not sure where or why we abandoned need as a reasonable reason to marry, but I'd like to suggest its reinstatement. The idea that we're somehow supposed to be whole on our own before we can be any good to anyone else seems to me a big lie (not to mention a flop, in terms of results). Whatever marriages looked like back in the '40s or '50s, before all this self-actualization started, it can't be worse than what they look like today, when we're all trying to be the entirety of everything, flailing and failing.

In the Old Testament book of Ecclesiastes, King Solomon muses about all he's seen in life and what the pieces seem to mean. (Or not mean, as the case may be—his conclusion is that most of what he's valued is meaningless.) But he writes convincingly of the benefits of doing life together, rather than going it alone:

> Two are better than one, because they have a good return for their work: if one falls down, his friend can help him up. But pity the man who falls and has no one to help him up! Also, if two lie down together, they will keep warm. But how can one keep warm alone? Though one may be overpowered, two can defend themselves. A cord of three strands is not easily broken.

This was the belief Steve and I built our marriage on, one with which I think Madeleine L'Engle and Louise Rich would have agreed: we're stronger together; we're more than the sum of our parts. And it's not just the two of us here, caring for the furnace and the dog. God is the third strand in our cord, the one who wove us together in the first place, the extra strength we need. It sounds all spiritual and metaphysical, but for us it's the hope we lean into again and again when we sense that we might be coming undone at the ends.

I was listening to Sheryl Crow's *Wildflower* album when I wrote those lines above about needing each other. Her songs struck me as the strangest, most grim expression of happiness I'd ever heard. Supposedly at the zenith of her career, her romance in full bloom, she penned a group of songs about searching, being lost, not understanding…and being fairly certain the news would be bad if she did. It broke my heart, even before Lance Armstrong broke hers.

As I looked at my past, and my own failed romances, hindsight offered an awareness that might have been helpful back then: Relationships don't fail because they're cut quickly through with a knife or a pair of sharp scissors. Most come unraveled. A tug at one thread that twirls it slowly away from the others, getting caught on something that pulls you away. If marriage is like a sweater, life can often feel like a giant patch of thistles, thousands of tiny hooks reaching out to catch on and pull at the fabric until it's destroyed. The promise the Bible offers seems to be resistance to these hooks. We still walk through them, but they can't catch us in quite the same way; there's hope of emerging whole.

Chapter 3

That's Just Swell

I BLEW UP LIKE a puffer fish the minute we got married. I think you can even see a difference in our wedding pictures — how as the afternoon went on I just swelled up and up and up. On our honeymoon, I held steady — the Turks and Caicos were hot enough in June to guarantee that every act of marital union left us panting like aerobics instructors — but once I got home and took up the task of becoming this sexy new wife, my body embarked on some sort of bizarre expansion plan, filling our small condo like a fish reaching for maximum capacity in a new bowl. It's as if somewhere inside I thought, *If I take the place over, he can't kick me out . . .*

Ten pounds . . . fifteen pounds . . . twenty pounds. I outgrew my new lingerie. I broke down and bought new jeans, fearful that the old ones, lycra-enhanced though they were, would burst at the seams. I prayed for the strength of my zippers. I bought a new outfit on a Tuesday morning to wear to a friend's wedding; by Saturday, it no longer fit. Dozens of mood-setting candles remained unlit as I hid under cover of darkness, anxious to fulfill my wifely duty to my husband, but afraid that if he saw me, he wouldn't want to bother.

I heard a married pastor talk about the importance of giving your husband "redeemed images" to keep in his mental file folder: snapshots of you, his wife, naked and enjoying time with him. "Men are so visual," he said. "If you know he's going to have pictures of a naked woman in his mind, don't you want those pictures to be of you?" I wanted to give Steve these sorts of images, but I was so convinced that my extra pounds made me unsexy that I swung to the opposite extreme to protect him; for about three months, I don't think he saw much more than the occasional elbow or ankle.

I didn't know why all this was happening, but I had a hunch: I'd spent the past fifteen years in a constant state of hope and fear, wondering when and if some mysterious Mr. Right might finally burst forth from the ether and have me as his wife. I'd cycled through endless romantic disappointments, always the girl with the nice-looking boyfriend who couldn't close the deal. Looking back, I see the tension I carried: defensive explanations about why I was still single, unrelenting hope that today might be the day when I'd meet HIM (or if I thought I'd met HIM, that today he might finally call). I'd been my own 24/7 workout, wondering and worrying about when my prince would come. Not the healthiest mind-set, but it sure kept me thin. Now, that tension was gone. My prince was here, pulling me in for a hug whenever one of the Red Sox made a great play and whispering suggestions about a postgame celebration. For the first time in my adult life, I was relaxed. And bigger every day.

⟞⟝

"I know your secret!" a girl at church whispered to me. "When is the baby due?"

⟞⟝

We enrolled in our church's marriage course, and took a test to determine our "Love Languages." We talked about what made us feel loved, and how we liked to show love to each other. The point was, I think, how often the two miss each other—how most of us love others the way we want to be loved, missing a chance to give them what they really need. I thought back to law school, when my parents helped me get my first car. It was a used Volkswagen Jetta, and before I came home to pick it up, my father washed and waxed it by hand. My dad is not the most outwardly affectionate guy (my sister and I still warn him, "Look out Dad—we're coming in for a hug!" just to see the panicked look on his face), and so the image of him out in the yard polishing that car until it shone made me realize how much he loved me. It still does. In the book's terms, this means my primary love language is Acts of Service, which is great, because Steve is the epitome of the "How can I help you?" guy. A sense of security washed over me as we discussed this, and I reveled in the knowledge that we knew how to love each other well. I turned to Steve and asked, "How about you? What made you feel loved in your family?" confident I was up to the task. Steve was raised by three generations of Italian women. I should have seen this coming...

"Food," he said, a faraway gleam in his eye. "I remember my mother making my favorite food at night, and how much I looked forward to coming home." I smiled brightly, like this was a wonderful answer. Inside, though, I panicked.

The sad truth was, despite my expanding waistline, I couldn't cook. In the back of my mind I could see millions of housewives wagging their fingers at me accusingly, shocked by my lack of facility in the domestic arts, asking, *Don't you know that the way to a man's heart is through his stomach?* Honestly—I didn't know. I'd shunned my mother's valiant attempts to teach me the art of homemaking. I'd been cocky, arrogant in the way only a teenage girl can be, certain I was destined for something bigger and better than housewifery, and completely oblivious to the fact that even two-career power couples need to eat. When I first set out on my own, I was culinarily lazy, ending my days with a quick sandwich, a bowl of macaroni, or some random assortment of leftovers abandoned by one of my roommates. I'd never learned to cook meat (I tried to make a pot roast once with my sister; I hadn't seen the little piece of blood-soaked paper underneath the meat, so it simmered there at the bottom of the pan for three hours at 350 degrees). And despite our culture's growing foodie obsession with things like curries, port wine reductions, and scallions imported from Costa Rica, I cooked only when I had to; it wasn't important enough to me to take the time to learn. But because it was important to Steve, now, it was important to me.

Family members rallied to my aid. They bought me cookbooks

with "EZ" in the title, and sent links to websites that promised to teach me to make yummy, nutritious meals for my family in under thirty minutes. My friend Kristina bought me a yearlong membership in the Cooking Club of America. But I was missing basics these resources assumed. I didn't know how to quarter a chicken (what sort of knife did one use to cut a whole bird in four pieces?) or braise a roast, or deglaze a pan. I could boil water, toast bread, and scramble the occasional egg. I missed the days when I could have friends over just for beer and pizza, when hospitality wasn't equated with steaming food on a table. Before long, I hated dinner with a passion previously reserved for pantyhose and tow-truck drivers. Now that I had to engage food, the whole world had turned up the volume, it seemed, and I had to think hard about which foods I was going to engage. I did so, in frustrated fits and starts, for the next five years.

The Bible is oddly silent on issues of food and weight. I guess in a nomadic society where they were fed by manna that fell from the sky each morning, obesity wasn't an issue. Determined to be the proverbial wife of noble character, I dove in to recipe books and cooking shows, certain it couldn't be all that hard. I was an educated, intelligent woman; I'd learned to read and think and analyze all manner of complex issues. I should (in theory at least) be able to add heat to a protein, starch, and vegetable, and turn them into a meal.

I devised a plan: each night I'd apply the few basic seasonings in my repertoire to a different package of creature parts from the meat and fish aisle in the grocery store. I'd seen enough *Rachael Ray* to know that the beginning of all healthy cooking is a frying pan doused with olive oil, so that's where I began.

Monday we had steak (fried in olive oil, seasoned with salt and butter), linguini, and frozen green beans.

Tuesday I made pork chops (fried in olive oil, seasoned with salt and butter) and served them with fettuccini and frozen peas.

Wednesday was seafood night, with salmon (fried in olive oil, seasoned with salt and butter), on a bed of angel hair pasta with a side of frozen corn.

On Thursday I overcame my horror of poultry (really, who ever thought to eat the first bird?) and prepared chicken breasts (fried in olive oil, seasoned with salt and butter), with penne and frozen carrots.

Friday, I declared pasta night and served two heaping bowls of spaghetti with garlic (fried in olive oil, seasoned with salt and butter) and sauce from the jar.

This was, incidentally, the week we discovered that Mylanta gelcaps are the best antacid on the market. Steve spent each evening making a weird "a-hem" noise, trying to clear the grease from his throat. "Really Love," he said after each attempt at a meal, "that was delicious."

Everyone said it would get easier, that I'd get the hang of it in no time. I waited, frustrated, wondering when no time would arrive.

༺ঙ৫ঙ৹

A month before our first anniversary, we threw caution (and condoms) to the wind and decided to start our family. I couldn't wait to be a mom, to see a new little person running around with our green eyes and Steve's cleft chin. I didn't care that our condo was only 600 square feet (including the closet) or that in all likelihood we'd have to convert Steve's giant hockey bag into a crib. I loved the family we'd created so far and was ready to welcome new members. And at the same time as all these joyous thoughts careened about in my head, I imagined another (unsung) benefit to reproduction: it would fend off fat comments for at least nine months.

⌒◌⌒

A few months later, I was still fighting fat on fat's terms, my stomach loose and jiggly rather than taut and indicative of new life. I was stunned by how much this bothered me, how ashamed I felt as I caught myself again and again forgetting to suck in my stomach. I developed an array of cover-up techniques to negotiate life in public: holding a pillow on my lap when I sat on a couch, buying sweaters and fleece pullovers in a size too large, not washing my jeans so they'd stretch. More discouraging than my weight gain was the energy I expended thinking about it, worrying, trying to hide what I'd become. I longed to tell everyone I met, "I don't know how this happened...this isn't who I am..." At some basic level, I no longer felt like me.

I threw money at the problem, joining a fancy gym and hiring a personal trainer; I worked out hard for months and lost three pounds. Pictures of me from our first Thanksgiving show my eyes swollen almost shut, my pants stretched to the point of bursting. I knew something was wrong, but I had no idea what it was.

I read the story of a former bodybuilder who had ballooned up to 585 pounds. When she went to a facility to get professional help for her weight problem, their first response surprised me: They didn't take away carbs, or fat, or dairy; none of the usual culprits we think about in the diet wars would come up for another three or four chapters. The first thing they removed from her diet was salt.

Salt.

It was a *Eureka* moment. Here was something I could try to turn my ship (with its newly broadened stern) around. But at the same time, I couldn't imagine life without salt. I loved salt — quite possibly more than I loved sex. Ice cream could live for years in our freezer without me even thinking about it, but a bag of potato chips had a life expectancy of under twenty minutes. A few shakes on a sandwich, soy sauce on sushi, garlic salt on popcorn — my motto was, *If some is good, more is better.*

In a surge of hope and motivation, I threw away all of our salt: I emptied the three shakers (even the pretty pewter one in the china cabinet we never used), tossed the soy sauce in the trash. After that went the garlic salt, the meat tenderizer, the bouillon cubes. I gave amnesty to the mustard on the grounds that it was a condiment in its own right, but baloney and the Cheez-Its had to go, along with my favorite granola (that featured sea salt as a key ingredient). I wrapped up the garbage bag and took it down to the dumpster behind our condo to keep myself from digging through the trash to feed my addiction.

For about fifteen minutes, it felt great. A new lease on life, a chance to get back to the version of me I hadn't seen for quite some time. But then I got hungry. And nothing — not a single thing save possibly one overripe banana lying abandoned next to the coffee maker — seemed worth the effort without salt. In that moment, I realized two things:

1. Almost everything I'd eaten for the past three years was really just a way for me to consume more salt; and

2. The people who say you can make up for the lack of salt by adding "other, more interesting spices" to your food are evil, two-faced liars. (The only company peddling more false promises than Victoria's Secret is Mrs. Dash.)

That first week was torture. I hated food, I hated my body. I hated the realization that salt was *everywhere*: my favorite fried rice, the refried beans we used to make tacos, soup. I caught a cold and was clueless on how to care for myself: no saltines, no Campbell's Chicken Noodle. I think I recovered mainly because the prospect of even one more hour curled up under a blanket on the couch with a box of tissues and a cup of herbal tea (why would anyone make a sick person drink something that tastes like the lemon-scented cleaner you use to clean your bathtub?) was all too gross to bear. But if this would get me back into my jeans (and make me feel okay when Steve suggested I slip out of them) it seemed a small price to pay.

As it turns out, salt was only part of my answer, a small piece of this puzzle it took me three years to solve. The final piece came, eventually, from a bowl of popcorn. Not literally, perhaps, but in a metaphoric sense I'm embarrassed to admit. I was leading a small group of women who were curious about exploring the Bible and what Jesus has to say about what's possible in life. One of the women openly hated me. I'm not sure why she came (okay, that's not true: she came because her heart was broken by a guy who had just dumped her for another girl around the same time he was expected to propose and I was an easy target as she worked through her anger) but she was there, every

Tuesday night, telling me what I was doing wrong in any and every area of my life.

We had a movie night, gathering to watch (for a reason I can't fathom now) *The Sisterhood of the Traveling Pants*. She insisted on making popcorn: a fancy method involving a pot on my stove, three kinds of oil, salt, pepper, and cheese. She was right; it was delicious. And as I stuffed handful after handful into my gaping maw, I realized that this was not going to help me get on one of those commercials featuring sleek, successful dieters and their before and after photos. I mentioned my weight gain, pushing the popcorn aside.

"You know what you have to do?" said Popcorn Woman, in a tone that made clear she planned to tell me, whether I wanted to know or not. "You need to spend all your workout time on cardio until you achieve your desired weight. Then add strength training, but not before." I looked at her with thinly veiled disdain. She was lying. Everyone knows that you need to add muscle mass to burn more calories, I thought. She's trying to sabotage me. Which just seemed mean, given that Popcorn Woman was almost six feet tall and that perfect type of angularly slender, elegant rather than gaunt. What did she know about being five foot four and almost as wide as I was tall?

Six months and as many new pounds later—the group long ended and Popcorn Woman moved back to the cold northern climate from whence she came—it occurred to me to try her suggestion. I'm not sure why; perhaps I was just bored by the endless ineffectual sets of lunges, squats, and push-ups. I decided to do all my workouts on the treadmill and elliptical machine, just to see what would happen.

You can guess the rest: after about three months of eking out a sweaty, painful mile and a half each afternoon at the gym, the weight melted off like so much butter in that woman's popcorn pan. My face re-emerged from the puff, my eyes were clear again, and my jeans—oh my grateful, happy, longsuffering jeans—breathed a sigh of relief as they were freed from the duty of stretching to the last inch of their capacity to keep my lower half covered. It was like a little miracle, delivered by an angry, hurt woman who still cared enough to tell the truth, knowing that I probably wouldn't believe her. It made me think of a passage in the Bible exhorting us to entertain strangers, because we never know which one of them will turn out to be God's angel in disguise.

Chapter 4

Give That Man Some Sex

"GIRL — YOU'VE GOT to give that man some SEX!"

This was the single best piece of advice we received in our newlywed year. It came from a conference video on which a female pastor, newly married herself at the age of forty-eight, was speaking to a roomful of married couples and pulling no punches about what it takes to make a marriage work. She looked straight into the TV camera and said (right to me, it seemed), "At the end of the day, your husband doesn't need deep conversation...he needs you to put on a thong and *work it!*" Then she talked for a full half hour about "stewarding" a collection of lingerie.

Steve and I spent hours pondering her suggestions. Was I brave enough to hide my underwear in his laptop before he went to work? Could he surprise me with a path of rose petals leading to a bubble bath, given the almost certain probability that our dog would eat the flowers and need an emergency trip to the vet? Suddenly, sex seemed complicated, something requiring a master plan (not just a wink, a smile, and half an hour). We weren't sure what to make of that.

From the time we returned from our honeymoon, people who knew we'd waited to have sex until after our wedding asked (with big, enthusiastic smiles), "So—did you and Steve just rip your clothes off and devour each other once you were finally married?" Rather than admit the truth, I went for enigmatic, on the theory that restraint was the better part of valor. Because as much as I wanted to paint a raucous picture of us tearing up our honeymoon suite in repeated fits of unrestrained sexual gymnastics, the truth is, neither of us remembered all that much about the first time we "knew" each other in the Biblical sense. (This might have been God's way of protecting us, as writers are known for revealing things we'd do well to keep private. Suffice it to say I can share what I remember without worrying that my family will learn details they never wanted to know.)

Our wedding reception (which was highlighted by the inadvertent playing of "Have Yourself a Merry Little Christmas" over the PA system and an unplanned first dance to the longest, slowest version of "I Only Have Eyes For You" in human history, after which I sequestered myself alone in the ladies' room for a full ten minutes, stared at my wedding dress in the mirror and squealed in unrestrained glee, "ThankyouthankyouthankyouthankyouGod!" until the bathroom attendant walked in and interrupted my party) wrapped up around 3:00 p.m. We went with our photographer to the beach and took pictures of Steve and me running in and out of the ocean—which felt spectacularly rebellious, what with me in the most expensive gown I'd ever owned and Steve in his rented tux—then we made our way up to our wedding suite, giddy and exhausted. We'd survived the grueling obstacle course that is wedding planning: racing to meet a UPS truck next to a pile of mulch at a nearby garden center to stop our invitations from being shipped back to Minnesota; getting our money back for rings that had turned from white gold to brassy green; fending off the evil bridal consultant who told my sister to stop breast-feeding her baby so she could lose weight before the wedding...we were ecstatic to have all that behind us. After the wedding, we knew, came special privileges. But that night we were almost too tired to think about them.

My thoughts were unromantically practical: I was hungry, and the inn did not have room service. Which meant that Steve and I needed to change out of our wedding gear, soon. It seemed absurd to grab my jeans and head into the bathroom to change, but crass to break our happy moment with a blunt, "So, should we get this over with now so we can go get some food?"

We sat on the bed together, talking over the day and looking out our window at the river. A giant sailboat glided past on its way out to the ocean; a seagull landed on the deck and preened in the glass reflection. Another wedding started on the grounds below, the bride on her father's arm walking toward her smiling groom. I felt a wave of relief that I wasn't her, that Steve and I had made it to the other side and were finally married, finally alone. The fact that she still had to stand through an entire ceremony and then dance for hours at her reception seemed almost cruel to me (which is a funny way to look at things for a girl who'd spent the past fifteen years longing to be a bride).

As we watched the wedding, Steve unfurled the complicated web of my hairdo. He pulled out fifty-seven pins before losing count, then ran his fingers through my hair. The bride and groom enjoyed their first marital kiss, after which we followed through on ours...

Then we went to dinner.

Okay, I remember slightly more than that. Let's just say that I was smiling that night at the restaurant as I ordered a chocolate martini to toast life with my new husband. But here's the important part: at no point did I think that our first time together was supposed to be the zenith experience of our sexuality. It was a beginning, not the arrival. We'd waited to make love until after we were husband and wife not because we believed God would supernaturally give us all sorts of wedding night techniques to astonish one another (although I suppose that happens—perhaps I should ask around?). We were after a different promise: that rather than the stereotypical experience where a couple has great sex before they're married, then watches somewhat helplessly as the quality and quantity of their intimate life plummets precipitously for their remaining years together, we'd see a different sort of trajectory to our sexual happiness. I was fine if sex was just functional at first (and I won't lie—I'd prayed mightily that it would be functional), because I believed the promise in the Bible about how God's people go "from glory to glory"; that life experiences get better as we pursue them with God, according to His plan. The rules in the Old Testament seem explicitly designed to facilitate this: "If a man has recently married," it says in Deuteronomy, "he must not be sent to war or have any other duty laid on him. For one year he is to be free to stay at home and bring happiness to the wife he has married." While I couldn't imagine Steve marching into his company's HR department to demand this particular employee benefit, I loved the implication that great sex was something we'd get better at over time. That seemed like a promise worth investing in, something a couple could build a fun life around. But at the same time, the world around us seemed littered with land mines threatening our new structure.

⚬≋⚬

"He's leaving," Anne said in a flat, monotone voice I barely recognized.

"Who's leaving? What do you mean?" I asked.

"Joe," she explained. "He no longer wants to be my husband. He met a woman in an online chat room, an old girlfriend from twenty years ago. What am I going to do?"

Over the next twenty minutes, she described how Joe had told her of this latest development in his romantic life the way other men might describe a fortuitous spike in their stock portfolio, making it sound as if his decision was obvious, like he had no choice but to reopen this relationship because gods of the internet had brought him and this woman back together in so *serendipitous* a way.

Anne prayed fervently for her husband in the weeks that followed—we all did. It was like he'd lost his mind, developing a vivid fantasy life about how perfect his existence would become if only he could be with this other woman. That this new life would require him to leave his wife and two young children and move 1,958 miles away was inconsequential. He had his eyes on a prize and he was going for it, and it didn't seem to matter who got run over in the process.

What went wrong? I talked with Anne about this, Monday-morning quarterbacking their marriage as we looked for signs of where he'd started to unravel. Her libido had disappeared a few years earlier, she told me, mysteriously erased in the hormonal avalanche of new motherhood. "He said he was okay with it," she marveled. "He said not to worry—that he'd never want me to do something I wasn't in the mood for. As it turns out, though, he was lying." She went on to share the behind-the-scenes truth he'd admitted on his way out the door—how rejected he'd felt in those sexless months, how frustrated and detached and angry he was as their baby replaced him and took all of his wife's love and attention. "Twenty minutes of sex a couple of times a week might have saved my marriage," she lamented. "But I was too busy waiting to be in the mood to see what was really going on."

This wasn't the only problem, of course. There were other tensions, other issues they'd swept under a whole bunch of carpets hoping they would go away. They hadn't swept them away because they didn't care, she explained carefully (defending him more than he deserved, I thought, but hey, it was her marriage and she got to decide when we pulled out the "I Hate Joe" T-shirts and when we put them away)—they both cared. But caring hadn't led them to the solutions they needed. They'd had no idea how to bridge the growing gap between them, what to do with the pile of tensions and disappointments. Talking didn't help the way all the books promised. Neither did sharing their feelings while trying to avoid accusatory language. "The truth is," she told me, "communication isn't all that helpful when neither one of you has any idea how to fix what's broken."

This got me thinking. We're smart women, most of us; we know how to pick up basic social cues in most situations. How have we concluded that when we say, "Not tonight honey, I don't feel like it" and our husband walks away, it's really okay? On the surface, it might look like men just switch their attention to *SportsCenter* or the *Wall Street Journal*, but I wonder if we're not a bit delusional in our insistence that this is a cost-free transaction in our relationship?

In an interview actress Kate Hudson gave *Vogue* after her son was born, she described how important it was for her to tend to her husband — their intimacy, their sexual connection — and not get caught up in other things. "If this doesn't work," she said, "then my family is broken." I cut out her wise words and posted them on our bulletin board. Later, she and her husband divorced. There were rumors of other people, but by all accounts (at least those I read in subsequent issues of *Vogue*) they had the most amicable of all marital endings, and were raising their son more or less together... along with whatever new boyfriend and/or girlfriend happened to be on the scene at the moment. This struck me as perhaps the most terrifying destiny I could imagine: single, raising a child mostly alone, wondering if my latest Mr. Right Now will still be around next week, while watching my former husband woo some other chicklet as we all sit around a big Christmas tree opening presents.

These stories sent me into a panic, and what happened next was grim: in a mad rush to become my husband's ultimate fantasy girl, I came a bit unhinged. I was determined to put out on demand, like cable TV. I plotted out positions and poses, wanting to keep things "hot" between us, like the magazines say you have to. But here's the thing: I'm not the most coordinated girl on the planet. I can't really multitask. So night after night as I twisted myself into various impossible positions while swinging from the light fixture and saying, "Go Baby Go!" I was always on the brink of tears, certain that one wrong move would leave us in a heap on the floor checking for broken bones, my work as a master marital seductress a failure. Deep inside, I was riddled with fear, worried that if I didn't figure things out, Steve would become like Joe, or Kate's ex, or one of those men Naomi Wolf described in *New York* magazine, his mind wallpapered with porn images of other women he'd seen in magazines or online. It wasn't the best frame of mind from which to captivate him.

I thought about sex constantly. Not in a fun way. More like the way you think about airplane crashes before boarding a cross-country flight. I thought about the clash between Cosmo-style sex—positions and outfits and five new tips to drive him wild—and real life sex, the kind that's messy and passionate and often kind of awkward. I thought about a quote that said, "God is the author of this mystery, so nothing you will ever learn about sex will make much sense without Him." I waded through the Song of Solomon (the "sex book" in the Bible) frustrated by the poetic metaphor. It said that Steve would graze among my lilies, and that at some point I'd have a belly button filled with wine. I had no idea how to apply such tips in real life. And the more I thought about sex this way, the less I wanted to do it.

Jesus didn't talk about sex all that much. Mostly, he went

around forgiving people who had messed up their sex lives, setting them free and exhorting them to "go and sin no more." One gets the sense that these encounters were more than counseling sessions; that when Jesus straightened out your sex life, you had his power to live differently from that point on if you wanted to.

But in one parable, he suggests an alternative view of the idea of investing and seeing return. That got my attention, perhaps because it didn't seem — on the surface, at least — to be about sex at all. He tells a story of a man who gave his servants money before leaving for a trip, saying, "put this to work until I come back." When the master returned, he called the servants and asked for an accounting. The first servant had invested the money, earning a return of ten times its initial value. He was rewarded with more to invest. The second servant also put the money to use, reporting a slightly lesser return; he too was commended and given more. But the last servant handed back the same amount he'd been given. He'd been afraid of losing it — of the punishment he'd receive if his investment went badly — and so he hid the money, pulling it out only to return to his master. The master was *not* pleased by this protectionist approach. He took the money and gave it to the servant who'd invested most aggressively. Reflecting on this, Jesus says, "I tell you that to everyone who has, more will be given, but as for the one who has nothing, even what he has will be taken away."

This passage is usually invoked in sermons about finances, or about not wasting our talents just because we're afraid we'll fail. But when I heard it quoted a few Sundays after our wedding (and just a few hours after the "You've got to give that man some SEX!" video) I had one of those *"Aha* moments" Oprah always talks about. What if this applies to sex? I wondered. What if it was a "talent" God gave me, something I could invest to build our marital intimacy? "To everyone who has, more will be given..." The words turned over and over in my mind. Remembering the wise counsel of that woman preacher, I decided to *give that man some SEX.* Steve had promised to be faithful unto me; the least I could do was provide some "unto him" when requested.

I turned to a book that I'd read before we were married, *The Power of a Praying Wife.* I vaguely recalled seeing advice in there about having sex when you don't feel sexy; I flipped through the pages to find it.

"When your husband communicates to you what he has in mind," the author said, "don't roll your eyes and sigh deeply. Instead, say, 'Okay, give me fifteen minutes'...During that time, do something to make yourself feel attractive. For example, take a shower or a relaxing bath. Put on scented body lotion or his favorite perfume. Comb your hair. Wash your face and prepare it with products that make your skin look dewy and fresh. Put on lip gloss and blush. Slip into lingerie you know he finds irresistible. Don't worry about your imperfections; he's not thinking about them...While you're doing this," she continued, "pray for God to give you renewed energy, strength, vitality, and a good attitude. Hopefully, when you're ready, your husband will find you worth the wait."

I was dubious. Perfume makes Steve sneeze, and I couldn't see how a little extra blush on one set of my cheeks would hide my self-consciousness at the size of the other. Did I want my skin to look *dewy*? But prayer — that I could try.

"Lord, help me love my husband," I asked. "Help him want to love me. I don't understand how he can want to make love to me when I look like this, but when he does, help me want to." Tired of the extra effort of pre-sex primping and perfume, I turned to a well-known commercial for inspiration: I decided to be like Nike and *Just Do It*. Even if I didn't climb up on the chandelier; even if no lingerie was stewarded. I figured that some must be better than none, and I wanted Steve's some to come from me.

As I rolled toward Steve at night rather than away from him, I found that more often than not, once we were a few minutes into our time together, I enjoyed myself. Some of these nights were not the stuff you read in the pages of men's magazines or even romance novels—the phrase *utility sex* comes to mind. But it comes to mind for a reason, acknowledging that this sort of sex is useful sometimes, it serves a purpose.

I was also surprised by the results outside our bedroom. Now, when Steve pulled me in for a hug or a long kiss, I could relax into it; I didn't worry that he was hinting for something more. Knowing he could have sex with me whenever he wanted to freed him up to lavish me with affection at other times; the two were no longer intertwined. And our interactions—watching TV, driving to the mall, walking the dog—took on a fun, sexy tone. When I felt particularly self-conscious (which was often) I'd pray for God to make Steve miraculously find me attractive, and to be extra affectionate. Those were the nights when Steve would come home and mention how beautiful I was—how a certain T-shirt made my eyes look extra green, or how glad he was that his wife had some "junk in the trunk." Those were the nights when he couldn't seem to get enough of me, or lavish me with enough attention. I couldn't explain it, but I didn't argue.

Later, Steve and I moved into a new condo and painted our bedroom. It was another inside joke we had from that marriage video, about a passage in Song of Songs where King Solomon describes his marriage bed as *verdant*. "That means," the pastor clarified, a big smile on her face, "you have lots of great sex and your marriage is alive!"

We wanted our walls to be green.

Chapter 5

Little Foxes

HERE'S A CONFESSION: I didn't understand how some of my friends remained blissfully unbothered when their husbands or boyfriends brought home *Maxim*, went to strip clubs with the guys, or watched women's beach volleyball on ESPN for entire Sunday afternoons. "He can look, he just can't touch," was the prevailing sentiment, as if a man's lustful lingering over some other woman couldn't possibly harm a real, 3-D relationship.

It struck me as no coincidence that these were the same friends who obsessed endlessly about their body fat, asking again and again if they looked okay in their new jeans (then refusing to believe me when I said yes). It made sense, in a way—if I dressed every morning next to a picture of a woman painted head-to-toe in Ultra Tan and then airbrushed to Barbie-esque proportions (whose come-hither look I'd just seen my husband ogling), the odds of my feeling great about myself—or Steve—seemed pretty low.

There was this idea out there, some unanticipated vestige of the women's movement, I guess, that "evolved women" should be okay if our boyfriends or husbands perused the Victoria's Secret catalogue or spent too much time arguing the musical merits of the Pussycat Dolls. Apparently I missed that elevator to the top floor of womanhood, because I'd always felt threatened when the man I loved looked at other women the way I looked at new shoes. There was never once a moment where I was "okay" with this — it's just not how I'm wired. Before, I'd thought this was my *problem*, something I needed to work on to achieve peace or inner wholeness or enlightenment. It never occurred to me that I should trust my instincts, or that my aversion to sharing my man's mental space with other women was a gift from God, a sign that my internal compass was calibrated correctly.

King Solomon, one of the wisest men in the Bible, wrote pages and pages of observations about life. He had it all: the respect of his people, more money than we can fathom, a wife he loved. But in the end, he blew it. In his old age, he allowed himself to be seduced by foreign women, turning away from God to worship his new wives' idols. In doing so, he took down his whole nation. What's helpful about his story is that he wasn't one of those grizzled Hugh Hefner–type guys who thought things were going just fine. He knew he'd blown it, and wrote about what he learned in the hopes that the rest of us might make better choices.

I dove into his wise words, looking for help in negotiating this maze. What I saw surprised me: Solomon was amazingly candid about the threats to marriage. "Catch for us the foxes," he implores his new bride, "the little foxes that ruin the vineyards." His Proverbs were filled with warnings about the dangers of seductive women, going on and on about the importance of avoiding their treacherous, deceptive snares. "Delight yourself in the wife of your youth," he tells husbands, "may her breasts satisfy you always." (It went without saying that to remain forever satisfied with my breasts, Steve was going to need access to them.) There were, I noticed, surprisingly few passages in the Bible cautioning against the dangers of seductive *men*. Part of me railed at this bit of gender inequity, but at the same time, I couldn't think of a male equivalent on the radio for that song that asks, *"Don't you wish your girlfriend was hot like me? Don't you wish your girlfriend was a freak like me?"*

"God," I prayed, "help me see the foxes."

Our first fox showed up just a few weeks after our honeymoon. A woman at work began lavishing Steve with attention. They'd always been flirty, he admitted, but she'd been dating some other guy for over a year, so he'd never thought much of it. "That's just how Jessie is," he said.

This bugged me, and even more so once I met her. I knew this type of girl. She was beautiful, in the way that revealed how much time and attention went into making sure compliments always flowed her way. (Do you know what I mean? How some women are the exact opposite of what we call "natural beauty," which is relaxed and casual? Like they have extra-attuned radar to pick up when people aren't paying them enough of the right sort of attention and adjust accordingly?) In her skin-tight wrap dress, four-inch heels, and long, highlighted hair, there was nothing casual or relaxed about her.

The first time we met, she was nice to me, lovely even. But she went out of her way to demonstrate that she'd known

Steve longer, and that because of this, they had special inside jokes to which I wasn't privy. As hard as I stared at my wedding band, reminding myself over and over again that Steve chose me, not her, I couldn't help it: I felt threatened. I thought of King Solomon's warning: *Beware of the seductive woman... She's waiting, determined to entice you... Her path leads down to the grave*, and a pop song I'd listened to over and over again in law school, by a singer who brought a different guy on stage each night at her concerts and sexually taunted him in front of everyone, singing lyrics about the things she'd do to him if SHE was his girlfriend. I'd always pictured myself as that singer, controlling men with my feminine wiles. But now that I was on the other side, with another woman dancing to get my husband's attention, those lyrics made my stomach churn.

A footnote in my Bible mentioned a woman named Jezebel in connection with all of these warnings. She was the wife of a king named Ahab. He'd broken his covenant with God when he married her, ignoring strict instructions to take a wife who shared his faith, rather than a woman who worshiped the primary rival god of that time, Baal. Worship of Baal was all about sex: orgies, fertility rites, the erection of giant phallic poles to mark the altars. And Jezebel's hallmark was seduction. Not for pleasure, but for power.

Jezebel wore the pants in the family. As you read her story, you can almost hear her grumbling, "If I didn't do everything around here, nothing would ever get done..." In a very real way, she's where the term "high maintenance" comes from. She killed God's prophets, rode roughshod over her husband, and ruled with a bloodthirsty determination to get what she wanted.

Jezebel lives on today, some believe, a grim spirit looking for women to invite her into our lives. She promises the results we crave: adoration, attention, control. And to a certain extent, she delivers. Jezebel is the girl who's first to flash the crowd at Mardi Gras or shows up dressed as a "naughty cop" for Halloween. She's the woman who compliments your husband at the company Christmas party for the brilliance of his work, then turns to you and says loudly, "Oh, good for you—you've *almost* lost all that baby weight!" She's the memoirist who is now married with two kids, but blogs about how much she misses the way she used to saunter into a bar in a tank top and no bra, just to bask in the chaos her presence churned up in the men around her. She's Glenn Close in *Fatal Attraction*, Rebecca DeMornay in *The Hand That Rocks the Cradle*. Jezebel's spirit demands attention, and she doesn't care who or what she destroys in the process.

Also, Jezebel is miserable.

There's a famous actress right now who epitomizes this. In almost every movie she does—even cartoon voice-overs—she plays the seductress. Her current partner is the second married man she's taken from another woman; his ex-wife is the epitome of the girl next door. He resisted some of her snares, refusing to marry her. So she had baby after baby to tie him to her. Now rumor is, they're married. And every so often, when her profile drops a bit, she leaks a tidbit out into the press about how she stole him from his former wife when they worked together on a movie: "We just had to be together," she gushes. "It was irresistible..." We tune in to see her latest exploits, drool over pictures of her endless offspring, laud her good works for an international charitable organization. She controls us. But not many of us think about what she represents...or how we'd respond if she showed up in our husband's office, making inside jokes.

⚜

Wow, he reminds me of Matt, I thought, staring at the bass player. Matt was an ex-boyfriend. I was at a concert with my friend Kelsey; she'd scored us fourth-row seats. The stage lights flashed, the music started, and I was swept away by the first song. My eyes were drawn to the drummer, who was playing with a big grin, and then to the bass player on the right side of the stage, who was holding the beat steady, eyes casting across the audience. *He really does look like Matt*, I thought again. I was suddenly aware how much sexier "Matt" was up on a stage making music than he'd been when I'd last seen him (lounging in his parents' living room waiting for me to drive him to court for a DWI hearing). I couldn't look away.

I spent the next ninety-two minutes willing myself to look at the drummer. Or the guy with the fiddle. Or the lead singer with the crazy hair and the long goatee. But my eye kept coming back to "Matt," wondering who he was, what his life was like, what it would be like to meet him. I imagined all of the qualities that had drawn me to the real-life Matt all those years ago, while all of the reasons we'd broken up were magically erased. I was having an extramarital crush, right there in the middle of the crowd. It was kind of fun. Harmless, I thought.

That night when I got home, Steve was in the living room. I'm not sure when we'd reached the point where we no longer stopped what we were doing when the other walked in, but

Steve continued watching the home improvement show he'd been focused on—something about draining pipes before removing an old toilet...just as I'd continued working on my laptop—something about uploading books to the latest social networking site—earlier that day when he'd come home from work. I tried not to think about how often a shift like this is found in the opening pages of divorce memoirs: *It wasn't that we hated each other...It's just that we'd become more like casual roommates than lovers.* I hated the fact that we'd become more casual roommates than lovers, but felt an odd inertia that kept me from doing anything about it. We merely exchanged basic updates, checking in from time to time from opposite ends of the couch.

After one such perfunctory conversation ("How was the concert?"/"Good") Steve turned back to the toilet draining show and I pulled out my laptop to Google the band. I wanted to know something about the bass player. What was his name? Was he married? Part of me hoped he'd have a website that revealed that he was a dork, or an idiot, or a repeat DWI offender like the real Matt. There was nothing, though. He was an enigma, which left me free to create him in my mind.

This, I knew, was dangerous territory. I thought of an essay collection I'd read in college by fellow Wheaton alum Nancy Mairs. The assignment had been to consider how Mairs had woven details of her increasing disability (she suffers from multiple sclerosis) into stories of everyday life. What I remembered more, though, was the way she'd woven hints of infidelity into those same stories, sharing how she and her husband had betrayed each other, again and again. She shared these painful highs and lows like they were normal, like they happened to everybody. And perhaps they did. But by the end of the book, I felt like one of those balloons that has lost its air, dangling pitifully, beaten by wind and rain. Now, searching the library shelves for that book, I found she'd written another volume, this one more open about marriage than the last. She echoed my building theme, but with words of warning:

"When I had been married for half my life," she said, "the whole rambling, precarious, cockeyed structure George and I had banged together almost toppled down around our ears." She admits that this wasn't entirely unpredictable, that they'd "had about as much chance of constructing a shapely and sturdy dwelling place as a couple of blindfolded children turned loose with a heap of toothpicks and marshmallows." She recapped how she'd had many affairs over the years, how the passionate high of engagement drew her to man after man for dalliances of varying lengths: "I loved...their capacity for waking me from the torpor into which my spirits habitually sank." The affairs, in her eyes, brought her back to life. But they involved little deaths, too, she admitted. Men didn't always return her attentions. Men left and went back to their own lives, making her realize that they'd never assumed responsibility for hers. But she believed herself powerless to resist.

That's how I felt that night after the concert: disappointed that I was no longer the sun around which my husband orbited, powerless to stem the tide of churning images about the bass player and who he might be. I wanted to be the center of attention, and he—the bass player, not Steve—seemed the most promising option. Jezebel. That's not good stuff to build on.

The rest of Mairs's book was dark and unflinchingly real. I'd been fishing for some bit of faith that had held her and her husband together, for a tangible moment where God had helped pull things back on track. But the reality was far less climactic: her husband just never got around to leaving. He'd threatened, made some plans, but seven or eight years later, he was still there. In the book's final chapter, she shared his cancer diagnosis, and her new fear that she'd outlive him, that she'd end her life suffering and alone. She wrote that she didn't believe in hell, but what she described sounded as close to it as I could imagine. I didn't want to end up where she was.

In the weeks that followed, I noticed something strange: now that my fantasy life had been opened, it was overflowing onto everyone and everything I saw. I found myself daydreaming about a guy on a reality TV show; I watched flexing muscles at the gym without ever considering the person they were attached to. I was hyperaware, suddenly, whenever one of Steve's friends was around, and I caught myself dressing up a bit, and doing funny things to get his attention. That's when I knew I was in trouble.

One day after a church gathering where I'd spent quite a bit of time trading funny banter with this friend, I looked over at Steve and felt like I'd cheated. It was sickening. I felt like I'd crossed a line somehow, done something from which I could never go back. (Steve, so far as I know, had no idea any of this was happening.) Part of me felt like an idiot for making such a big deal out of nothing: all we'd done was talk, and we'd spent the whole time surrounded by other people. But I know when I've done something wrong, even when the rest of the world might tell me it's no big deal. (Big deals start small, privately, inside where no one else can see them.)

When we got into the car to go home, I turned to Steve and said, "I have a crush on X! I don't want to. I don't know how it started. I don't know how to stop it. But I need you to know so it doesn't go any further. I'm so sorry..."

Steve, ever unflappable, pulled me in for a hug. I waited for him to say something. I tried to imagine what I'd say in his shoes: how hurt I'd be, how angry. But he's not me. He prayed, "God, thank you for bringing this to light. We ask for freedom here: freedom in Trish's mind and heart. In the name of Jesus, I bind the evil schemes of the enemy off of my wife's mind. I bind spirits of adultery, seduction, and manipulation...leave Trish now and go to the foot of the cross."

"God, I'm sorry for entertaining these thoughts," I added. "I'm sorry for flirting with X. I'm sorry for watching and thinking about other men. I don't want to do that anymore."

"Trish, in the name of Jesus, I pronounce you forgiven," Steve said, pulling me closer. "This has no hold over you," he reassured me, "it's finished." We talked about what had happened, retracing the steps that had led to my mental wandering.

"It seemed like such an easy way to get my needs met," I admitted. "It was less embarrassing to fantasize about some stranger than to admit to you that I needed more attention." Then I got really honest: "I figured that if I was worth it, if I was prettier or more interesting, you'd want to pay more attention to me. I just didn't want to hear you say that, so I never brought it up."

"That's not true!" Steve said, his eyes wide with surprise. "I love you, I love spending time with you. I just zone out sometimes. I don't ever want you to feel like you're not the focus of my attention," he added. "As your husband, it's my job to adore you."

"But all the books say I shouldn't need that—that I should be independent, and get all of my attention from God."

"That's stupid," Steve said firmly. "God sent me to love and pay attention to you. If I'm not doing that, then I'm not doing my job." I was surprised by the strength of his reaction.

I'd like to say it ended there. In some ways, it did. I stopped doing internet searches for news about the band and the bass player, and I lost the urge to flirt with X. But I'd forgotten how, once you open a door for sin (and I was spooked enough by these seemingly harmless situations and how thoroughly they took siege of my mind to be convinced that they were, indeed, *sin*) it's hard to get it all the way shut again. Foxes don't go away. They just get more crafty.

A couple in our church separated. No one really knew why. There was no betrayal in the usual sense. Word was, she was simply taking off, leaving him to pick up the pieces. My heart broke for him, and burned furiously at her—he was such a great guy, what was she thinking? *If Steve ever died*, I thought, Y *would make a great husband*... I shook my head, blinking, trying to toss the thought from my mind. And yet it seemed sort of harmless; practical, even. *I'm not thinking about marrying* Y *now*, I assured myself. *I'm thinking about how God might bring something good out of sad times if something awful happened.* I filed that away.

Suddenly, *Y* was everywhere. I hadn't noticed before how often our paths crossed, but it seemed like we were in all the same meetings, passing in hallways, exchanging e-mails about all manner of things we'd never discussed before. He went from being on the periphery of my mind to dead center, like a target. My divine GPS system went haywire, begging me to turn around, to repent, to change course. This time, though, I didn't. Not at first. I thought I could handle it on my own. Whenever thoughts of *Y* came up, I banished them. I reminded myself to think about other things. But *Y* kept popping up, his armor shining brighter because he was remaining faithful to his wife, still hoping to work things out. Still, I thought this was a battle I could win over time, if I just hung in there. The Bible promised that if I resisted the Devil, he would flee. That was my plan.

"I need to talk to you," Audrey said. There was an urgency in her tone. "I have to confess something. I'm having weird thoughts about someone in our church, and I can't seem to get rid of them."

"What sort of thoughts?" I asked.

"It's a guy. His wife left him. I keep thinking about how if Jack ever died, this guy would be a great husband."

I stared at her. "You're kidding, right?" I asked, knowing full well that she wasn't. "I know who you're talking about. I've been thinking the exact same thing." We were both silent for a moment, contemplating the weirdness of this conversation.

"Lord, forgive us," Audrey said. Then, looking at me, she explained, "What else can we do but pray? In the name of Jesus," she continued, "we take authority over these vile spirits of death and adultery that are suggesting these awful fantasies, and command them to leave now. Don't return," she continued, "you have no place here."

"Yes, Lord," I agreed, adding my own confession to the mix. "Give us thoughts only of our husbands," I asked. "Lead us not into temptation, but deliver us from every evil." (It was then I first realized the Our Father prayer covers a lot of ground—no wonder so many people pray it every single day.) And as we prayed, I felt something heavy leave me, like a lump that had been living in my chest dissolved. I looked up at Audrey; she looked better, too.

"That was wacky," she said. "I'm so glad I told you."

"Me, too," I agreed. We wondered how many other women in our church were wrestling with the same thing.

Audrey and I had two similar conversations in the months that followed. Each time we sent these pernicious thoughts to Jesus, we confessed and received forgiveness, we prayed for the lives we had, not the shiny fantasies Satan tempted us with. And each time, the lies went away, until the next time our guard was down and they'd try to come back. Jesus warned that this would happen. Foxes are persistent. They look cute and harmless when they're sneaking into your vineyard, but they'll tear things down in a heartbeat if you don't fend them off.

⟳

Steve and I went out to dinner with a couple we'd just met, Jasper and Helena. We swapped stories like old friends, feeling like we'd known each other for years. After dinner, we went back to their apartment for dessert, and were talking about a celebrity couple that had just split up, and how tough it must be to be faithful in such a crazy industry.

"Jasper was unfaithful to me once," Helena said, stopping

the conversation cold. "Things haven't always been like they are now." I stared at them, wondering what to say. Jasper sat by listening, unruffled, like this was the most normal after-dinner conversation in the world.

"It was at the beginning of our marriage," Helena explained. "A woman came along and we thought she needed the love of the church. But she wanted the love of my husband. We didn't pay close enough attention, and she snuck in and captured his attention."

I listened, spellbound, wondering how to reconcile this story with what I'd seen earlier that night: two people who were clearly in love, happy, and engaged with each other. They had two great kids and a third on the way. By any standard I could think of, they were thriving. How was this possible? Emboldened by Helena's honesty, I asked. "How did you survive? What got you through?"

"Our friends," Helena said. Jasper nodded. "We were in a church group with this incredible bunch of couples, and the men surrounded Jasper. They stayed up with him all night when he came clean, and they didn't let him wallow or back down from the consequences of what he'd done. They made him face the truth: how he'd betrayed me, how he'd violated our wedding vows. They made sure his confession was real, and thorough, and that every last bit of the evil he'd let in came out into the light." There was a pained look on Jasper's face, but he leaned into Helena, his arm around her, letting her speak freely. He was present, but never interrupted. It seemed like a story they'd shared before, something from their past, rather than their present. I didn't see how this was possible.

"What did you do?" I asked Helena. I wondered if she would turn out to be one of those wimpy doormats who forgave pitifully without thinking, or believed she deserved that kind of treatment.

"I cried, and I fumed," she admitted. "I was crushed. My father cheated on my mother, so this just seemed like one more piece of proof that men can't be trusted. It took me months to get over it," she continued. "I prayed and I prayed and I prayed to forgive him, for God to help me, for God to save us. I even asked God to help me forgive her."

I flashed back to the days after I'd learned that my college fiancé had cheated on me, how the anger came in layer after layer, seeming like it would never end. And how surprised I'd been by how mad I was at the other woman, even though she'd never promised me anything. There's something about the violation of the sisterhood—women stealing each other's men, rather than having their own relationships—that cuts deeply. And all deep cuts need healing, even when they're secondary to a larger wound.

"At a certain point," Helena continued, "I knew I had to reclaim the tangible parts of our life she'd tried to steal. I needed to define what was *ours*, and that meant taking back what had been *theirs*." I leaned in to hear more. "I went to every restaurant they'd ever met at and I prayed there," she said. "I prayed over every park bench they'd sat on, every road they'd driven down. I prayed and prayed and reclaimed these things for God, and for us. I asked for miracles. The Bible says that the marriage bed is undefiled, and I needed God to make that true for us, because I couldn't, and neither could Jasper."

"So something happened," I prompted her. "A miracle, I mean? Because it seems like you guys are fine now—I never would have guessed that this happened."

"I always dreamed of having a husband that was a spiritual leader," Helena said with a smile. "One who loved me and my children. But truly, I never imagined a husband and father as amazing as Jasper is now." She told me of a night recently, when she'd been up late with one of the kids and couldn't get back to sleep. "I was flipping through one of the Bibles we have around the house and I opened it up to Hebrews. It was the very Bible Jasper had used then, during what I call the Three Days of Death. It was marked up with a red pen, and at one point a line was drawn to the bottom of the page, pointing to the words he had written: *I am an adulterer.* My heart sank when I saw that," she said. "But at the same time, I was overwhelmed with thankfulness. My heart hurt for the man who wrote those words, for his great pain and revelation. But that is not the man I am married to now."

"Wow," I said. "That's incredible." Steve was silent beside me. Neither of us knew what to say, where to take the conversation next. I stared at Helena, looking for telltale signs of remaining pain or conflict between them. There were none. She was truly happy with her life and her husband. We were watching a miracle.

Which brought me back to Jessie, with her blown-out hair, tight jeans, and high-heeled saunter. "God," I prayed, "protect us from Jessie. Do whatever it takes—move her desk, her job, her house. Keep her away from my husband."

Tell Steve what you're thinking, He said.

"I can't do that! He'll think I'm paranoid." I pictured myself shrinking up into a ball of shame as Steve said that there was nothing to worry about; that he and Jessie were just friends. How could I tell him that I'd been dumped for more than one "friend" in the past? I knew how to tell Steve about my transgressions; it felt altogether different to suggest he might be set up for one, too.

Trust me, God said. *I'll cover you.*

I talked to Steve that night. It was awkward and embarrassing, and he looked utterly stunned as I described my concerns. I cringed, bracing myself for his dismissal of my silly fears, a knot clenching in my stomach. *We've only been married a little while*, I lamented. *How can this be happening already?*

Steve paused before answering. "At first, this seemed a little silly," he said. "But now that I think about it, you might be onto something. Jessie has always been overly friendly with me—I thought it was harmless fun. But it's hard to imagine how God's best for us could include me flirting with another woman. And I'd hate it if the situation were reversed. I'm going to avoid her," he concluded, as if this was the most normal thing in the world.

Conversations like this, and some of the choices we made as a result (canceling subscriptions to my fashion magazines that featured scantily clad women, not going out for lunch with friends of the opposite sex alone, switching to the channel that featured Senate debates during racy commercials) made us one of the most conservative couples in our circle of friends. We didn't mean to be boring or prudish. Just the opposite, in fact. We knew that to remain excited about each other, we'd have to resist the temptation to be titillated by every new visual smorgasbord wandering by. I read these words by Naomi Wolf about an experience that changed her perspective on marital intimacy:

> I will never forget a visit I made to Ilana, an old friend who had become an Orthodox Jew in Jerusalem. When I saw her again, she had abandoned her jeans and T-shirts for long skirts and a head scarf. I could not get over it. Ilana has waist-length, wild and curly golden-blonde hair. "Can't I even see your hair?" I asked, trying to find my old friend in there. "No," she demurred quietly. "Only my husband," she said with a calm sexual confidence, "ever gets to see my hair."
>
> When she showed me her little house in a settlement on a hill, and I saw the bedroom, draped in Middle Eastern embroideries, that she shares only with her husband — the kids are not allowed — the sexual intensity in the air was archaic, overwhelming. It was private. It was a feeling of erotic intensity deeper than any I have ever picked up between secular couples in the liberated West. And I thought: Our husbands see naked women all day — in Times Square if not on the Net. Her husband never even sees another woman's hair. She must feel, I thought, so hot.

Reading these words made me realize how happy I was with our choices, how secure they made me feel — not in Steve's perfect faithfulness (or mine), but in the knowledge that our marriage was valuable to him, and worth the effort of protecting, even if our choices made us a little weird. Weird was worth it. Because after all these awkward conversations about other women and couples who'd cheated and crushes on bass players and best friends, Steve and I discovered that we were closer than before. What might have come between Steve and me if we'd let it float around unacknowledged, now linked us together in a sexy sort of trust that added fuel to our fire. I was still overweight and unpregnant. I still couldn't understand how my friends could be okay with those magazines. I still hated the Victoria's Secret fashion show. I was still me. But with all of that out in the open, there were moments—when we accomplished something together, or solved some puzzle life threw us with both of our skills—when I felt, as Naomi might say, *so hot.*

Chapter 6

Seeds

A MONTH AFTER OUR honeymoon, we embarked on the strangest of all possible newlywed vacations, flying to Dallas, Texas, for the annual Seminar Convention of Mary Kay Cosmetics. Right before I met Steve, I'd become a Mary Kay Independent Beauty Consultant. I liked the money I earned selling lipsticks and eye shadows, and while there was a decided overuse of pink in the packaging, I couldn't deny that the three-part skin-care system made my skin look better than the water-on-a-washcloth plan I'd employed for the past two decades. Plus there seemed to be significant earning potential in meeting new women and teaching them how to apply blusher so their cheeks didn't look like Nike's trademark swoosh.

That week in Texas, Steve accompanied me on all manner of strange motivational adventures as we explored the Mary Kay dream. He sat through a four-hour dinner where women dressed in prom dresses sang "You Are the Wind Beneath My Wings" to one another and gave out awards of faux jewelry.

He smiled gamely during the "Pink Cadillac Dance" at an early morning team breakfast, even as a director draped him in a hot pink feather boa. He kept a straight face at the Mary Kay Museum, and then later that afternoon as we listened to a victory speech by a sales director who'd sold 850 eye creams as she worked her way through a misspelled acrostic about how we need to *perstevere*. I knew I'd be watching Classic NHL reruns for the next seven years to balance out this week of pink. And yet, as we sat through these events, we were caught up in an almost palpable excitement, the inviting sense of possibility that comes with being part of something larger than ourselves.

On Sunday morning, we skipped the tour of the manufacturing plant to go to church. We knew that The Potter's House, an African-American church led by the lively pastor/author T.D. Jakes, was somewhere in Dallas, and we didn't want to travel all the way to Texas without sampling Texas-style church.

As we walked in, we were greeted by people everywhere: "Good morning brother! Good morning sister! Bless you!" I'd never felt more welcomed in my life. "Turn to the person next to you and ask how you can be praying for them today!" the announcer suggested after the opening song. Turning to our left, we met M.J., an earnest man who was at least seven feet tall, who was praying for God to bring him a wife. "I'll pray for that!" I assured him before turning back to the front. A commanding woman took the podium, a serious look on her face. "We're a *family*," she said in an ominous tone. "We come together because we need help, and that's what *family* does." She told us to bridge the gaps between the aisles and join hands. "We're gonna pray right now," she intoned somberly. "We're going to call on the holy power of the living God..." My heart sped up inside me. Something about her words, and this place, and this gathering of people made it seem like God *would* move powerfully, like what we were doing *mattered*.

"We're in *trouble*," she continued. "We have all kinds of needs. We have people in our family who need to be healed, people who need to be set free from addictions, people who need to be saved from their loneliness and set in relationship with others who love them. Now you know what *family* does when someone is in trouble?" she asked. "We gather together. We close ranks against the enemy until things are *right*. And that's what we're doing right now. Let's pray to the Lord right now to *make things right...*"

All around us, thousands of people broke into prayer—for themselves, for each other, for the world. I asked God to bring M.J.'s wife, to heal my mother's breathing trouble, and to help our country, which seemed to be speeding toward disaster on more levels than I could keep track of. And as we prayed, I felt it, that sense of *family* the minister described. I'd felt it before, certainly—when my parents and siblings closed ranks around me when I was on the run from my first marriage; when my mom's eleven brothers and sisters gathered for reunions over the years and I was immersed in a sea of cousins too vast to contemplate. In a way, it was like what I felt during the Mary Kay pep rallies. But this seemed less fleeting. And it had a depth that made those pink parades seem like a pathetic counterfeit. This gathering had tangible power. *We are family*, I realized, looking around at all the faces that looked so different from Steve and me, as they looked back at us.

The next day, Steve and I spent four hours trapped in a plane full of exhausted consultants on the airport tarmac, grounded by a thunderstorm. One of my new friends asked where we had been on Sunday and we told her about going to church.

"I'm into spirituality, too," she shared. "I've been to psychics, and I believe in Feng Shui. But I've been having nightmares lately; I'm not sure what to do about that. I wonder if it might have something to do with my father who died three years ago. I mean, where is he now? Is he all right? Can he still speak to me?"

I mentioned how I'd experimented with Feng Shui and psychics, along with a whole host of other spiritual options, and how disappointed I'd been when they hadn't really helped me. "A big part of the reason I'm into Jesus now is that following him works so much better than anything else I tried," I confessed. She looked unconvinced. Just then we were cleared for takeoff, and she returned to her seat.

Later that week, I was praying about the Mary Kay conference, asking God what I should do with my new business. I sensed Him saying, *You have a choice to make. You can pursue Mary Kay and I'll bless that. Or you can be part of creating a church like what you experienced in Dallas. But you can't do both.*

I sent my inventory of nail polishes and hand creams back to Mary Kay headquarters, closing the door forever on all the excitement I'd felt while wiggling around to Natalie Cole singing her rendition of "Pink Cadillac" in Dallas. But in the weeks that followed, I couldn't stop thinking about the friend I'd chatted with on the plane. I felt like our stories were connected. Or like they should be. I realized that I wasn't the only one out there looking for spiritual answers to the big questions in life. I decided to write down my strange story, to see if it might open up more of these conversations.

⤙⊚⤚

Flashback: When I was a twenty-something law school student, overwhelmed and hating my life, I saw a New Age spiritual author interviewed on *Larry King Live* whose perspective on faith and relationships encouraged me. I found her audiotaped lectures at the bookstore, and I listened to them every day on my way to and from class. Eventually, I even got a job working for her. One day, as I pulled into my apartment parking lot and turned off the car, I sensed God saying to me, *You'll do what she does, only your source will be different.* I didn't know what that meant: Could I make a living encouraging people? Writing books and giving talks about how more is possible in life? Something inside me sang with hope for the first time in months. But what was my source?

This became—along with my quest for Mr. Right—one of the driving forces behind my spiritual search. I was looking for some path or another that didn't already have a bestselling name attached to it. *A Course in Miracles* had Marianne Williamson, Feng Shui had Lillian Too. The astrology market was cornered by the woman who wrote the *Sun Signs* books, and Sonia Choquette was everyone's favorite psychic. Julia Cameron had paved *The Artist's Way*, Neale Donald Walsch conversed with God, and after reading Wayne Dyer's vague explanations about manifesting my destiny, I couldn't see what was left.

Eventually, after a few years of searching, I made up my own path. It was an amalgamation of the others with some random thoughts of my own about what should be possible in life thrown in for good measure. I gave lectures and workshops, and ultimately wrote what I hoped would become a book about all these things. Filled with audacity, I called it *Feminine Magnetic Power.* Up to my eyeballs in denial, I became my own source.

I tried to sell this first book to publishers, in ways so decidedly dumb that it pains me to think of them now. I ignored all the advice in the industry, certain my work was *different, unique, special...* I eschewed query letters and proposals, sending gigantic bound copies (printed out on one-and-a-half-spaced pages, in a bizarre font I thought would draw attention) to the unfortunate agents and editors I'd highlighted in my dog-eared copy of *Publishers Marketplace.* I spent a fortune on postage. And a short time after I sent out my ocean of manuscripts, waves of rejection letters came back at me as if carried by the next tide. Each one stunned me with its summary rejection of my work. Did they even read it? I wondered. Now, of course, I know the answer, an unequivocal *No.* They didn't read it; no one would. I'd ignored all the rules of the profession, behaving like a self-declared protégé and predetermining my failure as certainly as if I'd never sent the doomed book out at all.

I put the manuscript away. I had a fight with my then-boyfriend about wanting to get married, even though I'd promised him repeatedly that I wanted nothing of the sort. I heard God tell me He had a husband for me, but I needed to take Jesus seriously, and felt that surge of ridiculous hope again, just as I had that day in my car in law school. I wondered how this might be possible, and knew I'd try just about anything if it was.

I spent the next year edging up on Jesus, attempting to ascertain what taking him seriously might entail. I went to a new church, I watched Christians on television, I cracked open my Bible for only the second time in my life and studied closely to learn what it said. I let myself get caught up in the fun and excitement of this new endeavor, forgetting my manuscript and trying to weave Bible verses into the talks I'd started giving about my assorted New Age practices. Then I received a phone call.

"Trish, it's Mary-rama…" my former life coach declared, drawing out the last note. (Mary-rama was a big fan of enthusiasm and anticipation, and did everything she could to create it. She ended every sentence with a lowered tone, like an ellipsis.) "I just spoke to my agent Paula about your book… She wants to see it… Can you send it to her…?"

Of course I could. Of course I did.

Paula loved the book. Loved the idea, loved the writing. She just wasn't sure she could sell it. "If you can get Jayme Brass to endorse it—or even better, write the foreword—then we've got a deal," she said.

Jayme Brass was the bestselling New Age author I'd worked for. I'd resigned when I realized that her personal life didn't line up with the spiritual promises she espoused, figuring that if she couldn't make this stuff work, who was I to think I could? Now, I had my doubts about approaching Jayme: for a teacher of spiritual love and universal oneness, she's not exceptionally forgiving of those she thinks have wronged her. I suspected I still had a place on her *persona non grata* list, despite the brief attempts I'd made to reconcile. We'd only spoken once after our falling-out, in the ladies' room at an event in Washington, DC. I'd given her my best wide smile and a hug, and told her how much I'd loved her most recent book. She'd eyed me warily, like a wounded puppy. That was the last I'd heard from her. I also wasn't certain about the spiritual element of asking Jayme to endorse my book. As hokey as it might sound, I wasn't sure how Jesus would feel about this trip down my spiritual memory lane. *I'm not following Jayme,* I rationalized as I typed her name into Google and scanned the results for her whereabouts, *I'm just reconnecting.* With utter naïve optimism, I thought, *maybe she'll want to learn about Jesus, too!* And just like that, I'd covered my questions with the evangelism blanket, certain that not only *should* I contact Jayme and ask for her help, it was my *Christian duty.*

That's when I saw the article. It was a longish interview with an online magazine about spirituality and politics. I scanned through Jayme's answers, pat responses I'd heard repeatedly when we'd traveled together. But then she veered off into a different story, something I'd never heard before: "Certainly, I believe in Jesus," she said. "In fact, I think that in another life, I was one of the women who walked with him, that I was with him at the crucifixion." I stared at the screen. She thought she was one of the women who walked with Jesus? Seriously? This was a different Jayme, much farther out on the ledge of wild ideas than I'd ever seen her. She'd alluded to her belief in possible past lives before, that was standard New Age fodder, but she'd never placed herself in history, never claimed a position of import in that way that begs the question: why does no one ever remember being a *chambermaid* when they tap into their past life?

I couldn't do it. Jayme had ducked around a corner with this comment, and I couldn't follow her, not to get an endorsement, not to tell her about my new friend Jesus, not for anything. I shelved my manuscript again, this time for the final time.

"Maybe it's a test," my friend Will offered when I told him, my eyes filled with tears of frustration. "Maybe it's like Abraham with Isaac on the altar? You know," he added gently, since I was new at this at the time and wasn't familiar with all the Bible stories, "Abraham — he and his wife Sarah waited for years to have the son God had promised. Then Isaac was born, and it seemed like a miracle. But then God asked him to sacrifice Isaac, testing his faithfulness. Abraham took Isaac, placed him on the altar, and was ready to kill him when God called, 'Abraham — stop! You've proven yourself faithful!' Maybe God just wants to know that He's more important to you than being published. Maybe if you put your book on the altar, He'll give you your dream back later, in some way you don't see yet?"

"Maybe," I admitted grudgingly. "But I'm not sure I believe that." Inside, I was quite sure I didn't, that this was just another in a long series of things God had taken away from me. Not for the first time, I thought, *Jesus is the worst thing that can happen to a girl...*

I was wrong. The day would come when I'd think he was the best thing that ever happened to me. But I couldn't see it from there, or even imagine it.

❧

Fast-forward two long years. Now I'm a newlywed, awash in the miraculous tangibility of realized prayers. I have a new name, a new home, and a new sense of identity, and I spend my days watching in awe as God supernaturally knits Steve and me together, as we each begin to blur around our individual edges, forming a distinct, clear *one*. Where before this would have terrified me, it thrills me now. Tired of the old me, I shuck her off like a down coat after a long winter, running headlong into the freedom and promise of this new life.

Writing became my job. I typed at my laptop all day, dredging up memories of every guy I dated, every spiritual dead end I wandered down. Some made me laugh, a few made me cry. Seriously, I thought, how did I ever believe that a purple pillow and a fish tank were the keys to my future happiness? Slowly, the chapters came together: my Catholic childhood and how I started to pray because of Judy Blume's book *Are You There God? It's Me, Margaret*; my first boyfriend in junior high school; the fiancé who cheated on me in college; the rebound man who pieced me back together only to rip me back apart in law school...on through to my elopement—on the eve of my thirtieth birthday—to a man with a few anger management problems. Some days when Steve came home, I threw myself at him with unbounded glee, thrilled to be living out this piece of my dream writing full time about all God had done for me. Other days, the ones where I'd spent nine hours immersed in how bad things used to be—my stupid choices, how blinded I was by sparkly jewelry and a grim determination not to be the last girl left standing in this game of marital musical chairs—I threw myself at him in a different way, begging him to talk to me about something normal, happy, different. "Remind me that I'm not that person," I asked. "Tell me that part about how I'm a new creation and the old can't haunt me anymore..."

This time, I researched the business side of how books get published. I learned that memoirs sell on proposal, and that I wasn't supposed to write out all the chapters and send them off to unsuspecting agents, but rather home in on the key facets of each chapter and pull them together into a marketing plan, complete with an analysis of competing titles and where my book would fit into the current array of options competing for readers' attention. I read agents' blogs and learned that when they say, "We only represent historical fiction (or sports memoirs, or cartoon books for the children of pirates)" they mean it.

Months went by. I wrote. I prayed for guidance about approaching an agent, and all I heard from God was, *Not yet.* I'd done the dead-end agent chase before and didn't want to waste my time on fruitless effort again, but it was increasingly awkward negotiating social situations in our highly motivated city, where every third person wanted to know what I was doing to make my plan happen. Even among our Jesus-ey friends, there were only a handful who didn't roll their eyes when I said (for the fourteenth week in a row), "I'm waiting to hear from God."

When finances got tight (read: we reached the point where we were making choices between bread and vegetables at the grocery store) I went back to work. The only job I qualified for, with my law license long since expired and nothing else but waitressing on my resume, was as a temp at the biotech company where Steve worked, floating between different administrative posts. The pay was better than I'd expected, and I was surprised by how much I enjoyed being back in the world interacting with office mates on a daily basis. Not to mention the overwhelming relief of walking into Target and realizing that we could afford new toothbrushes *and* deodorant, all in the same trip.

I didn't give up on my book dream. But I didn't do much with it, either. Then I read a memoir about another woman's succession of failed relationships and her attempts to make sense of them, and took note of her effusive praise for her agent in the acknowledgment section. The next day, I e-mailed that agent. She asked for a writing sample, so I sent her my draft proposal and waited excitedly by the computer.

Over the next two weeks, we had several long phone conversations. We analyzed different structures for the book, possible angles for telling the story. I reworked the proposal repeatedly based on her suggestions, each time hoping this would woo her enough to make her take me on as a client. "Are you my agent yet?" I asked one afternoon. We'd been on the phone for almost forty minutes and her tone had changed; it seemed like we were allies. "I'll let you know," was all she said. It was like dating, having my hopes dashed by the dreaded *Define The Relationship* talk. (I'd forgotten the maxim that if you have to ask, it's not what you hope it is.) "Give me one more revision," she said later that week. "I'm going on vacation, but I'll call you Monday when I get back and we'll discuss how to proceed." I sent her my revision Friday, then waited all weekend for what I hoped would be my big break.

Nothing Monday.

Or Tuesday.

Or Friday.

The following Wednesday I e-mailed her, asking something obvious like, "Do you think I should switch the section about my brother into the past tense?" just to reopen the lines of communication. This was the first of seven such e-mails I sent, none of which saw a response. I flashed back to a guy who'd broken up with me when I'd first gone off to college. We'd had a fight on the phone one Friday night and he said, "I can't deal with this right now. I'll call you Monday." Eight months later, he drove by me on the street of our hometown. I turned around and yelled, "Is it THIS Monday you're going to call???"

My cube job lost its luster, despite the toothbrushes and deodorant it allowed me to buy. What had looked like a stopgap when I thought I had a literary agent now held haunting shades of *this is your life*. I couldn't imagine how spending the vast majority of my waking hours making photocopies and sending faxes was what God had created me to do. It might have felt different if Steve and I had kids already, or specific goals like a big house or a dream vacation we were working toward. But we didn't, not yet. We just worked all day at jobs we weren't all that crazy about, and then figured out how to spend the money. That seemed like a lame sort of life.

The kicker was, we didn't have that much extra money. I read about a local writers' conference and longed to go, but the price would have put us back in that "bread or vegetables?" predicament from before. There was a chance it might be worth it — there would be agents at the conference, and even a chance to have lunch with some of them and pitch my book. I scrolled down through their bios, and a picture of a pretty blonde caught my attention — she looked like the imaginary reader I'd held in my mind's eye when I was writing.

"Elisabeth Weed is with Trident Media Group," her bio said. I read through the titles she'd represented, realizing that I had one of them on my nightstand. That seemed like a good sign. *Maybe I should go?* I thought. I pictured myself at a giant round table in a crowded hotel ballroom, jostling with all manner of other aspiring writers struggling to explain my memoir of how Jesus saved my love life. Even if we had the money, it seemed like an unlikely route to success. Then I sensed God saying, *You could e-mail her. That's free.*

Forty-five minutes later, I sent her a query letter.

She replied, asking to see pages. I sent them, not wanting to get my hopes up again, feeling slightly ridiculous for believing my story might be one of the ones worth telling. Here's what I didn't know: Elisabeth had just had lunch with an editor named Chris Park who said, "I'm looking for a book by a woman with an unusual spiritual path, sort of a *Sex and the City* meets *Eat, Pray, Love*. If you come across anything like that, keep me in mind." Chris was also a member of The River, a Manhattan church founded by a team from my church in Cambridge. She not only liked my story, she *got* it—she understood the wide gulf I'd jumped from more generalized spirituality to Jesus, and was excited about how it might inspire other women trying to do the same. Chris made a fabulous offer to buy my project, and suddenly, I was an *author*—I had an agent, an editor, a book contract with a deadline. And a reprieve from life in the cube.

Two years later when that book, *He Loves Me, He Loves Me Not: A Memoir of Finding Faith, Hope, and Happily Ever After*, was published, an e-mail from my Mary Kay friend appeared in my in-box. "I've been wanting to tell you something," she wrote. "The day we talked on the plane changed my whole attitude toward spirituality. I stopped going to psychics, because every time I went, it made me scared and unhappy. I stopped doing Feng Shui for the same reason. I'm not yet where I want to be spiritually, but I feel like God is working in my life. I'm trying out a Bible study, so we'll see how that goes. Thanks for being so honest; I just wanted to let you know that it helped."

In my mind, I saw a picture: I was wearing a green apron, selling tomato plants to aspiring gardeners at the beginning of spring. I sensed God speaking, explaining what I saw: *The person who sells the seeds and plants doesn't call her customers later to see if they're taking care of them,* He said. *She knows that some of them will be planted, and the ones that are watered will produce fruit. But there's no way to know which ones will take. It's not her job to worry about that. Her job is just to make the plants available, and to trust Me with the rest.*

Chapter 7

The Trouble with Multiplication

I SPENT MY COLLEGE years at Wheaton College, a small New England campus founded in the mid-1800s as a school for women. Like so many of its time, it was steeped in traditions handed down from one generation to another, legacies of a bygone era tinged with sentiment and symbolic meaning. Some of these traditions were funny, such as the belief that if you walked around the pond three consecutive times with a boy and he didn't ask you to marry him, the proper recourse was to push him into the water. Others involved *a cappella* singing groups welcoming new members at midnight, or sophomores creating colorful "gardens" from stolen freshman toothbrushes. (There was also the tradition of one neighboring school to paint the frog mascot of a certain fraternity a new color every time one of their guys deflowered one of our girls...) But the most revered tradition—the one prospective students were told about before they even had a chance to apply—was about entering the chapel: how only seniors could enter through the front door. This wasn't formally policed, of course—our campus security was too busy finagling donuts from the cafeteria ladies to stand guard over our version of Buckingham Palace. But as though we each had some internal monitor placed in us the moment we matriculated, no one I knew ever violated this hallowed precept.

I think I understand why. This small honor was something we had to earn. It wasn't a case of being in or out, but rather a marker of where we were on the journey. It was presumed that we'd get there eventually, but there was nothing we could do to rush the process. Our job was to complete each of the tasks set before us, our eye on that prize until we joined the thousands of women before us who had accomplished that goal.

The first time I walked through those doors as a senior, I felt different. It made *me* different, this acknowledgment that I'd earned my way to the top of the school's academic ladder, and was thus poised to jump off (up, one hopes, but who knows?) into the real life we'd been talking about for the past four years. It was like Alice, going through the looking glass. Things were different on the other side.

∞◎∞

"I can't do this anymore," I whispered to Steve, tears filling my eyes as we moved off to the corner. We were at a housewarming party for our friends Ben and Theresa, surrounded by no fewer than seven expectant couples comparing notes about gestation websites and maternity ward tours. At that point, Steve and I had been trying for two years to earn that kind of tour. We'd prayed. We'd fasted. We'd had dozens of friends lay hands on us and beg God to open my womb, but it hadn't happened. I'd gone to my ob/gyn to ask about various types of scientific intervention—specimens deposited in Tupperware to be inserted in me via yards of plastic tubing—only to find myself reading Peggy Orenstein's memoir, *Waiting for Daisy*, in the waiting room, a chronicle of how her years of similar treatment produced no children but almost wrecked her marriage. We didn't think that was the route for us, but yet we were caught in a vicious cycle, waiting and hoping, waiting and hoping, only to be crushed month after month when we still weren't pregnant. Did I do something wrong? I wondered. Was there something we'd missed?

"I don't know what to do," I told Steve that night at the party, "but I can't keep going like this..." Across the room, a newborn began to wail, and I saw seven women touch their stomachs in anticipation, each looking forward, I imagine, to the fast-approaching day when their own child would cry out for them.

At church one day, our pastor Dave suggested that faith, at its essence, means believing that God is always good to us. I loved this definition at first. It felt right, synching up with my optimistic, anything-is-possible outlook that drew me toward spirituality in the first place. I was a firm believer that present circumstances didn't define future possibilities, and I'd seen God come through in so many unexpected ways that I was always the first through the door in my "God Is Good To Me" T-shirt.

But over time, our infertility felt bigger than my T-shirt. It didn't leave me questioning whether God was *good*, per se. That felt beside the point, almost like biting into a vegetable and asking "is this carrot moral?" or petting my dog and wondering about her philosophy of life. Who knew? I believed God was good in a general kind of way: that He's big, and magnificent; that He created us in love, wants what is best for us, loves being in relationship with us across the wide span of our lives. But now, it felt like He couldn't always be trusted, like following Jesus might be a bit of a crapshoot, where I had to choose my prayers carefully because they wouldn't all get answered. I never said this to anyone, but I felt caught in the three-wish dilemma of finding a genie in a bottle, wondering if I'd misspent my wishes.

During these months, every woman I know who wanted a baby had one (this sounds like an exaggeration, but it's not): My editor. My agent. My two closest friends, their two closest friends, and even three couples who'd sworn they never wanted kids. Our friend Emily called one day in utter disbelief, announcing that she was pregnant with their fourth child. "We were on birth control!" she exclaimed, laughing. "But I guess if God wants you to have a baby, He makes it happen." It felt like God was taunting me: *See—I can get anyone pregnant, whenever I want to.* Which left me, with my regular as clockwork periods and Steve's adventurous willingness to try whatever position/timing/schedule might work to get me knocked up, out in the cold. I couldn't understand why God wouldn't open this door, and some days it was tough to remember where I left my "God is always good to me" shirt.

I wondered strange things: had I wasted too many prayers asking for parking spaces in downtown Boston, or for God to *please* help the dog do her business quickly on cold winter mornings so we could go back inside? God answered those prayers. Now, as I faced the possibility that there might be an economy to prayer, parking and quick dog poop seemed like dumb things to ask for. I thought of the time I prayed for encouragement one gloomy morning while walking from the subway to my office temp job. An hour into my day I was summoned into my boss's office and given a special award by the company president for excellent service (excellence at what, I wasn't sure, as all I did was sit at my desk and wait for someone to need something photocopied...). They gave me a sterling silver Tiffany key ring, complete with company logo charm that looked surprisingly like a stick figure of Jesus on the cross. *I'm refining you,* God said to me that day when I thanked him for the encouragement. At that moment, I was sure that He heard me and cared. Now, I couldn't reconcile such personal attention over a sad day at the office with the way my prayers for a child seemed to fly right back at me like boomerangs. It was as if God relocated without a forwarding address.

Steve and I both hail from bloodlines where reproduction is more a tide to be stemmed than a drought to be prayed over, and yet we felt like we were standing in this big field God had given us, looking up at a cloudless sky. Well-intentioned friends tried to hide their doubt about our chances, but I could see the calculations circling behind furrowed brows: *If she was thirty-five when they married, then by now Trish must be at least ___.* That's usually when they'd talk about how much joy I must derive from my dog, or make some comment about how great it was that I'd given birth to a book. Sometimes, I'd nod and smile politely at these comments, because that's just my style; I'm not big on confrontation. But other times I'd blurt back in frustration, "From what I've read in the Bible, God brings real children to women who ask. Not just books or girls who need to be mentored. I'm holding out for that."

It was exhausting, feeling both behind my peers in this new stage of life, and like we were the only ones who believed that God would do the things He promised. It seemed so much easier to resign myself to settling, to make peace with my plight. It could have been worse: I had a husband, a career, and a sexy, fun marriage. And yet it was these intricate, unexpected ways God had answered my prayers for love and career that made me reluctant to disregard all the promises in the Bible about how he brings children to women who think all hope is lost. I mean, it says, directly and specifically, "He gives the barren woman healing; she'll dance for joy as the mother of children." How could I argue with that?

Sometimes, when people prayed for us to get pregnant, they'd include their own agendas, asking God to remind us that He makes families in many different forms. "Maybe you'll have lots of *spiritual* children," one young woman suggested, happily dooming us to life without the blood connection to legacy that the Bible seems to promise. This idea seemed to comfort *her*, that my sole purpose in life might be to serve as a trusted mother/big-sister stand-in for people in need of a surrogate. But it didn't comfort *me*. It made me feel roughly the same as when I was single and well-intentioned folks had suggested that perhaps *Jesus* was the husband I was looking for, and wasn't that wonderful? I couldn't figure out why people of faith so often encouraged each other to settle for something—an answer, a solution—that didn't fit their longings? Was it because we're so uncomfortable with waiting? It's awkward, I admit. I hated when people asked whether or not we had children — partly because it hurt, but mostly because it was difficult to watch someone I barely knew wrestle with my disappointment. And yet part of me thought that if you asked a thirty-nine-year-old, obviously childless woman if she and her husband want kids, you've brought it on yourself: it's a pretty small group of folks who have decided not to reproduce. The rest of us are left rolling around in bed at different times of the month, wondering "Maybe I'm ovulating now?!" and hoping something will come of it.

In the late 1990s, Christian recording artist Rebecca St. James came out with a song called "Wait for Me." Written in response to Josh Harris's book, *I Kissed Dating Goodbye*, it was a plaintive cry for her future husband, asking him not to settle for anyone else, but to trust that someday, God would bring them together. If you're a Christian woman of a certain age, this song is more likely than not etched somewhere in your mental hard drive (if you follow any other life-management philosophy, chances are you've never heard of it). I thought of this song one night as I watched the Disney movie *Enchanted*. I was captivated by Princess Giselle's firm certainty that her prince would come to rescue her from her exile in Manhattan. She was absolutely sure, and argued down anyone who tried to persuade her that she'd better start figuring out how to make a life for herself on her own. She, like Rebecca, was okay with waiting. I wondered where she got that quality, as I didn't seem to have it.

I'd never waited gracefully. The closest I'd ever come was a sense of numb detachment when it hurt too much to keep hoping. I'd seen people who claimed to be waiting peacefully, but most of them had sharp edges around their eyes, tiny signs that they were scared, too. I didn't believe them.

The truth is, I never thought I'd have to wait or hope for pregnancy. My biggest fear had always been that it would come unbidden, before I was ready. I remembered my father remarking once on how odd it was that none of his four aunts ever had children (two adopted, but none gave birth). He hoped that my sister wouldn't have that problem, as she was tall and lean, like his side of the family. Nobody worried about me — I'd had childbearing hips since the sixth grade. Given my boy-crazy tendencies, I think there was more concern that I'd multiply before I'd finished learning algebra. I could almost hear the collective sigh of relief when I crossed over into adulthood with my flat stomach intact. After that, everyone assumed things would happen in their proper time. The good news is, Meg had no trouble getting pregnant, and her skinny hips did just fine in the delivery room. It's my hips that remained untested.

I saw singer Steven Curtis Chapman on *Larry King Live*. He, his wife, and his three oldest children were talking about the recent death of his five-year-old daughter, who'd been killed in an accident when their son hit her with the family truck. It was a devastating story, but what struck me, aside from the power of their faith, was the sense of *family* they shared, there at Larry's desk. The five of them propped each other up — emotionally, spiritually, even physically — in a way that came from being related to one another, from spending days and weeks and years under the same roof. In my experience, you can't get that any other way. There are other types of support, certainly;

solace is not limited to blood relatives. But there's a way in which parents and siblings know each other that is unique, unspoken, and solid. It was tangible, there on the video screen. They were in this awful thing together, and somehow they'd get through. *Steve and I might never have that*, I realized. The feeling left me raw. Part of my dream of having a family was, of course, cute green-eyed babies. But there was another, bigger thing I hoped for, and it's what I saw in the Chapman family: I wanted our children to have each other. To have siblings that knew who they were as little kids, who could corroborate how Steve and I succeeded and failed as parents and as people, who would encourage each other to remember gifts that might fall by the wayside, and know what it meant to be from our family. This was, to me at least, what it meant to leave a legacy. As excited as I was about the possibility that future generations might pick up one of my books and find some glimmer of hope, it seemed even more valuable that there be children who could reflect back and say, "Mom really lived that—here's what it looked like in our house..." As my sister once described it, when we sat down for dinner, it didn't feel like all the places around our table were filled.

Three friends had miscarriages within weeks of each other, one ending up in emergency surgery. I was grateful to be spared that pain and heartache, yet in some small way, I envied them. At least they'd gotten pregnant. I read the Gospel of John, where he describes how Jesus makes this point four different times in three chapters: *Ask anything in my name and my father will do it for you.* So I asked, again. And then I got my period. I saw the movie *Juno* and spent the next week fighting the urge to cruise our local high school to see if some young girl with a basketball stomach might be carrying a missing member of my family.

One night Steve and I were walking through the mall and a couple passed by with a beautiful newborn in a stroller. I lost it right there outside Banana Republic. My heart shut down and my eyes welled up and I just wanted to scream at God for being such a cruel, awful Father. Steve stopped and grabbed me.

"Listen to me," he said, taking my face in his hands, ignoring the people passing by. "We're going to be okay," he said. "I want *you*, I want *us*. Our marriage is more important to me than having children. I don't want to lose you to this. I don't want to see you feeling like you've let us down, or God has let us down. I love who we are, and if this is all we ever have, then that's enough for me."

I stared at him, stunned. My husband is Italian, and very devoted to family. All of his close friends had had children; I'd seen how he was with them. I knew how much he wanted to be a father, and what a great dad he'd be. "What will we say when people ask us about kids?" I asked.

"We'll tell them what I always do," he said with a smile. "We're doing our part. It's up to God to do His."

We gave up, at least in theory. We were still having lots of sex, each of us quietly hoping for a miracle. But I put away the thermometer, and stopped doing internet searches on the best way to pinpoint ovulation. We talked about adoption, but it all seemed too daunting—the red tape, the fees we couldn't pay—and we realized how unlikely it was that any birth mother would look at the profile of a couple who lived in a tiny one-bedroom condo two doors down from a housing project and say, "That's where I want my baby to be raised!" We gave up on that, too.

Our decision wasn't spiritual. Spiritually, we were baffled. The Bible was clear: children are a gift from God, and married couples should be primed and ready to go forth and multiply. Night after night we'd gone forth, but our one plus one still only ever equaled two. I put on more weight, which led to more awkward conversations with friends who thought I *was* pregnant. My four-year-old niece grabbed my chest one day and asked, "Why do you have breasts if you don't have a baby to feed?" At some level, our decision to give up was born of my inability to field these questions. And yet I couldn't fathom how the word "barren" could apply to me, or how God's promise that I'd dance for joy as the mother of children got lost in transit. I didn't understand how I could do everything right, and still not be able to earn my way through that door.

Chapter 8

The Secret

I WAS IN A BOOKSTORE CAFÉ one day, ostensibly working on my manuscript, sitting across from a special display devoted to books and DVDs from the latest power of positive thinking craze. I'd read parts of one of the books, enough to see that it wasn't all that different from similar books I'd explored over the years, pages filled with intriguing advice about how life tends to go poorly for people who insist that their glass is half empty. I didn't disagree. But as I looked this book over, pondering the hidden mystery it claimed to reveal, I couldn't help but remember that however encouraging those types of pep talks had been for me in the past, they'd never delivered on their promises: thinking positively and affirming what I wanted were never enough to fix the broken parts of my life. Still, I wished that they would. Even now, I wanted life to work that way.

I watched the people who stopped by the display: so many of them looked like different versions of me. Not literally, perhaps. Certainly I've never had the wherewithal to make my hair look as good as the blonde soccer mom who scanned the jacket copy while her daughter danced around singing, "You've got a secret, you've got a secret!" But the Jennifer Aniston look-alike in the Ann Taylor suit who kept reaching for the bare ring finger on her left hand with her thumb, as if hoping a ring might appear? We could be sisters. Same with the chunky Italian girl with too much eyeliner and a T-shirt that claimed she didn't care if she lived or died. Even the older man with the deliberately casual attire of someone who has just had the crap kicked out of him by an unexpected divorce and can't believe he's back on the dating scene. I felt like I could jump into the "How did we end up here and what the hell do we do to fix it?" conversation with any one of them, and we'd be sharing stories for the next three hours.

These folks — the ones seeking spiritual answers there in the bookstore — were my people. I spoke their language; I understood how baffling it was to have life fall out from under you just when you thought you were finally getting things up and running. In fact, sometimes I felt like I was still right there with them, baffled and searching, hoping someone would tell me what to do next.

Driving home, I thought about the book, wishing I'd bought a copy. Maybe it would help? The book represented a quick solution, and that's what I wanted. It seemed easier to flip through a couple hundred pages of pithy words about turning lemons into lemonade than to admit the truth: that despite my delightful, happy marriage, and a life that was humming along better than I'd ever dreamed possible, a few too many things had piled up on top of me. I was — for lack of a better way to put it — depressed.

I prayed, asking Jesus if I should go back, if maybe it was the pick-me-up I needed. *The book isn't wrong*, he said. *But it's only half of the equation.* He was right, I knew: I'd long since discovered that while there's tremendous power in lining up what I say with what God says in the Bible (for example: that I'm blessed, rather than cursed; that Steve will delight in me always rather than looking for a newer model; that God has a plan and a purpose for my life and that if I keep pressing forward through tough times, I'll see it), there's more to navigating the spiritual world than an *abracadabra* and a few well-chosen affirmations. I knew that this book wouldn't tell me anything I didn't already know. Still, though, I wanted it to.

I shouldn't have been surprised by the depression. My emotional life had always been a bit of a roller-coaster ride, with hopelessness and optimism duking it out for my allegiance for as long as I could remember. I'd be going along fine, and then suddenly be flattened by a voice in my head (a cold, slimy voice like Hannibal Lecter's) saying things like "Why bother?" and "You don't really believe this will work, do you?" Then the hope would leak right out of me, and I'd be left in a puddle of flat, grey despair.

In my twenties, I'd found a strange sort of solace in these dark days. My life had been a series of hopeful starts and bad endings; the fact that my mental health more or less paralleled these ups and downs seemed like the lone sign I still had some grip on reality. (As Cloris Leachman said to Téa Leoni in the movie *Spanglish*, "Sometimes, your low self-esteem is just good common sense.") But that wasn't the case anymore. I'd changed my spiritual allegiances, given Jesus a try, and had drastic and undeniable improvements to show for it. I had faith in a living

God who cared about my life and communicated with me. I had an adoring, handsome husband, meaningful work for the first time in my adult life, and a cute, fun dog who wanted nothing more than to lie in a patch of sunlight in the same room where I typed. By any standard, my life was flourishing, and most days I was, too. But other days, I wilted.

They snuck up on me, those days. I'd be going along fine, writing a few pages, figuring out how to drown something in olive oil for dinner, throwing in a load of laundry and wondering how long Steve and I could put off cleaning the bathroom. I'd have a longish phone chat with my sister and make plans to get together that weekend with friends. I'd pray for people I cared about (and even some that I didn't). Steve and I would have great sex. Sometimes I'd even remember to floss. I'd spend the better part of a week thinking, "Thank you, God, that this is my life."

But there were days where I couldn't do it. Couldn't work up the energy for basic hygiene, or to think of anyone else, or engage Steve in anything more than a blank stare, as if asking him, "Who are you, again?" The laundry piled up in the closet and unwritten pages piled up in my head. I lost track of what I was trying to say, or why, or who might ever care. The bathroom remained un-cleaned.

I knew about this sort of depression. Its snaky tentacles wind all around and through my family, especially the women. Historically, my ancestors have followed one of two spiritual paths: they either found some sort of spiritual outlet that was meaningful to them, or they ended up alcoholic, delusional, or some vibrant combination of the two. I'd found my spiritual outlet, put roots down with Jesus. And yet here I was in the fog.

"Honey," Steve said firmly, "you need to fight this off." He prayed hours of blessing and protection over me, but he couldn't be there all the time. He never knew which version of his wife he'd come home to: the happy grateful Trish celebrating our great life, or the distraught and distant ghost who didn't have the energy to shower or get dressed. Concerned friends suggested antidepressants, but I shrugged them off. I didn't want to zone out just as my life was worth showing up for. I was afraid pharmaceuticals would make me feel worse instead of better, functional in a corporate cube worker kind of way but too numbed out to hope. And if things got worse, I wanted some sort of fallback option.

Back when I first wandered into church, a new friend gave me a Bible with God's promises highlighted in blue ink and alphabetically cross-referenced in the back. As a girl in crisis, I'd appreciated these easy-access features to get me to God's hope as quickly as possible. And I was surprised how much they helped. "Lord, bless me indeed," I'd prayed. "Enlarge my territory." Shockingly, it worked. But as things got better, I mercifully forgot how bad they could be. Now, during one of those afternoons when I felt that sense of "Why bother?" pushing me back toward bed, I pulled that book out again, wondering if it could help.

I relearned to fend off nightmares by praying Psalm 91 out loud every night before bed: "He who dwells in the shelter of the Most High will rest in the shadow of the Almighty...if I make the Most High my dwelling—even the Lord, who is my refuge—then no harm will befall me, no disaster will come near my tent." I prayed the one hundred and fifty Psalms as if they were my own words, begging God to lift me out of the pit, hide me under the shadow of His wing, and then kick out the teeth of my depression until it slunk away in shame. I stopped watching TV shows where women were brutally murdered in their homes. I threw away a CD by a favorite singer because every lyric was hopeless and sad. But the best bit of advice I received came in the form of a question: "What if," Dave asked in a sermon one Sunday, "some problems are *spiritual*? What if there's more going on around us than what we see?" I read a book by Greg Boyd that talked about the battle between good and evil, about how we're caught in "the incomprehensible complexity of a cosmos engulfed in a spiritual war." Then I found Kathleen Norris's book *Acedia & Me* and saw that Dave and Greg might be onto something.

I'd requested this book from the library after hearing Norris speak at a writers' conference. It arrived six months later, by which time I'd forgotten all about it . . . and reached a panicked breaking point where I desperately needed to know what she had to say. I read three pages in my car in the library parking lot, then sped to the bookstore to buy my own copy to highlight, underline, revisit. It felt like the missing piece to a treasure map I'd been lost in, with the treasure being my happiness. I was writing a book about how my hopes had been realized in life, faith, and marriage. And yet there were days when I walked around in a fugue state, a cacophony of garbled thoughts crowding my psyche, all refusing to come to the surface for any sort of examination. *Who am I?* I wondered sadly. *What ever made me think I had anything to say?*

Acedia, Norris explained, is an evil spirit, somewhat akin to depression. But instead of being prompted by bad circumstances or body chemistry, acedia saps you of energy to care or participate in life. It has no obvious genesis. You're fine, and then you're not. Ancient monks and mystics warned against acedia's attack, placing it higher on the "problematic sins" list than envy, greed, or even lust. This caught my attention: first, that giving into this spirit was a choice, rather than something that just happened to you; and second, that it was more dangerous than lust. (I wasn't raised in Christian culture, but I spent enough time hanging around its fringes to get the impression that *nothing* was more dangerous than lust.) This acedia stuff seemed radical, and yet a perfect description of the inexplicable lows I'd descend to out of nowhere, in the midst of living my daily life.

I was captivated by Norris's description of her spiritual disciplines. She's different from me—she's a poet, a prolific writer, a spiritual seeker drawn toward a Benedictine order in which she is something called an oblate. She finds solace in repeating, together with Benedictines around the world, a daily liturgy of prayers and songs and time with God that doesn't pause if you have a mood swing or a bad hair day. Describing the days after her husband's death, she said, "I had not counted on the power of routine to provide a protective scaffolding." That caught my attention, making me think of an observation by actress Julie Andrews: "Some people regard discipline as a chore. For me, it is a kind of order that sets me free to fly." I needed, I realized, a bit of that sort of freedom.

I'm no stranger to routine. Every morning for as long as I can remember, the first thing I do is drink a cup of coffee and read some sort of spiritual book. My tastes have grown more refined over the years, transitioning from Taster's Choice to Starbucks, *A Course in Miracles* to *The Holy Bible*. But overall, my years of New Age training prepared me well for the practicalities of Christian life. Now, I can say with confidence, "Sure, I read the Bible every day" — because I always read the Bible when I have coffee, and until I've had coffee, I don't know what to do next. So if I'm up, dressed, and out in the world, that means I've had both caffeine and God added to my system to get me going. But all too often lately, I'd head out into my day after reading the Bible and forget everything I'd just read.

After reading Norris's observations about the power of routine to stabilize us, I cast about for ways to infuse my morning shuffle with more meaning, and a real connection with God. My friend Grace, who has five young kids and not much time to dilly-dally with meaningless spiritual projects, unwittingly handed me the key I'd been looking for: "At the beginning of my Bible time," she said, "I ask God, 'Show me the beauty in Your Word.' It's a paraphrase from Psalm 119, where the psalmist asks God for insight and understanding. I've borrowed it, because I don't have time to just go through the motions or skim a couple of passages to qualify as a good Christian. When I'm reading the Bible," she said, "I want to *get* something from it."

The next morning, coffee in hand, I opened my Bible to the page I'd marked with the little ribbon bookmark the morning before. It was in the New Testament, in the Gospel of Matthew. Jesus was about to launch into his famed Sermon on the Mount, perhaps my least favorite passage. (I've never figured out how to be comforted by his claim that I'm blessed when I'm poor, sad, and meek.) I had no recollection of reading the preceding pages yesterday, or what Jesus had said up to that point. "Lord," I prayed, already feeling discouraged, "show me the beauty in Your Word." On a whim I added, "Show me what You say about *happily ever after.*"

Then, out of nowhere, something happened. Ideas and insights came into my mind, almost like Jesus had come down off of his hilltop in AD 30 to hang out and help me find a new lens through which to see his words. He was there, in the words, speaking right to me. He began with some basics: *When you fight; reconcile. Don't lust after others.* Solid advice. Things got more complex after that, as he talked about my competing motivations: *Give to the needy, but not just to make yourself look good. Pray, but not just to make yourself sound good. Fast, but not just to make other people think you're good.* And then: *You'll be tempted to worship money, thinking it makes you more than you are. Don't, because it doesn't.* All true.

Then he got down to the nitty-gritty: *Don't worry...God knows what you need...Seek Him first and all the things you'd worry about will be given to you...don't judge others...with the measure you use, it will be given to you...don't throw your pearls in front of pigs...ask, seek, knock...if you give good gifts to your children, how much more will your Father in heaven give good gifts to those who ask Him?*

I couldn't believe I'd never seen this before. I wondered: what could my life look like if I used these specific principles as a template to shape my perspective?

Around this same time, I watched Oprah Winfrey's big New Year kickoff show, where she confessed a forty-pound weight gain and strategized to get back to the version of herself she wanted to be. It was sad to watch her struggle—I like Oprah.

But I couldn't help but notice how much of what she said was exactly the same as what she's been saying over and over again for the fifteen-plus years I'd been watching: "I've got to learn again to love myself, to reverence myself, to value myself and put myself first. This year," she said, "I'm making myself my top priority." It sounded so wise. Or, if I looked at it from a different angle, so selfish. Some of it was good — she was planning healthy meals, adding resistance training and cardio back into her routine. (They showed her singing "She'll Be Coming Round the Mountain When She Comes!" while gasping for breath on her elliptical machine, reminding me of why I love her.) But if exercise and eating right were the answer, I thought, wouldn't most of us be happier by now?

She talked about how weight issues are actually love issues, and said she needed to give herself more love to get better. I was pretty sure that wouldn't do it. I was struck by something she shared about how a friend had asked her if she might be depressed: "I can't be depressed," she'd responded. "I know what depression feels like." "I don't know," her friend had said. "Something's off — your movements are slower; your responses are slower. There's a dullness about you. If I were you, I'd look into what that is. Because it seems like you're not there."

It seems like you're not there . . .

Acedia.

If she's not there, I thought, how can she love herself back into who she wants to be?

Manhattan pastor Tim Keller once observed that "the fundamental cause of evil in the world is the radical self-centeredness of the human heart." This rang so true for me when I read it that I copied it out longhand and posted it above my desk in my office. We're all selfish. We hate to admit it, but inside we know it's true. We all think we can rescue ourselves from the things that make us dull (or angry, or hopeless, or sick). But experience—mine, Oprah's, probably yours, too—reveals that this type of thinking is delusional. I used to think I needed more love—the love of a man, someone to marry me and take away my deep shame at still being single (my version of Oprah's deep shame at still being fat). And I did need that, just as Oprah needs to lose weight. But there was a link missing in my life, and without it the other things I tried to fix myself would never, ever work. That link wasn't self-esteem or spa time. The link was Jesus. Which is awkward, because most people don't want to talk about Jesus.

What would Jesus say to Oprah? I have no idea, really. But I knew what he said to me. He talked to me about fishing.

Of the four accounts of Jesus' life in the New Testament, John's is my favorite. He was Jesus' best friend, and a mystical sort of guy. He writes about how much God loves us, describing why Jesus came and how he interacted with people. In the final chapter, after Jesus has been crucified, died, and risen from the dead, John tells us of one more interaction Jesus had with his disciples. They'd been fishing all night, but caught nothing. Early in the morning, Jesus called to them (although they didn't realize it was him): *Friends, haven't you caught any fish?*

"No," they answered.

Throw your net on the right side of the boat, Jesus said, *and you will find some.*

When they did, there were so many fish in their net that they couldn't haul it in. At that point, Peter did a double take, realized that the guy on the shore was Jesus, and jumped into the water to swim to him. After pulling the net ashore, they all ate breakfast together, enjoying the miraculous catch.

The fish were cool, and the message about fishing on the right side of the boat wasn't lost on me (I'd spent years fishing all over the place, only to pull up a few tadpoles and the occasional flounder). I got the idea that Jesus would direct me to better choices if I'd consult him. But it's what happened next that caught my attention. Jesus turned to Peter and said, *Do you truly love me?* This was an awkward moment, certainly; their first real conversation since Peter had denied knowing Jesus just before he was crucified.

"Yes, Lord," Peter said. "You know that I love you."

Feed my lambs, Jesus replied. Then he asked Peter the same question two more times, with similar instructions. Then he said, *Follow me!* This was a moment of forgiveness and calling. Jesus not only forgave Peter for abandoning him, he reinstated him to a position of leadership. He called him to give up everything he'd been before, and step into something better. Seeing Peter at his absolute worst, Jesus forgave and transformed him into someone who could use his life to make a difference. And what a difference he made. Just a short while later, it was Peter who explained to the baffled multitudes what happened when the Holy Spirit came upon them at Pentecost. It was Peter who answered when the people asked, "What should we do?" "Repent," he said, "and be baptized every one of you, in the name of Jesus Christ for the forgiveness of your sins. And you will receive the Holy Spirit," he continued. "The promise is for you and your children and for all who are far off—for all whom the Lord our God will call." Peter was the guy God used to explain how a relationship with Jesus involved a new covenant, replacing the complicated system of Jewish law that had governed his entire life. And it's to Peter that God said, "this isn't just for the Jews, it's for everyone." Not bad for a guy who was a total dufus for the first part of his life, jumping out of boats, slicing people's ears off and otherwise being of no help to anyone. Following Jesus changed Peter. It's what gave him his story.

This is Oprah's dream, I think. I know it's mine. We all want our efforts to amount to something, to leave the world a different and better place because we were here. But like Peter, our faults and screw-ups (a bad guy for me, another bowl of potato chips for Oprah) trip us up again and again. At different points in our lives, this passage suggests, Jesus will stop by to see how things are going. *Catching any fish?* he'll ask, knowing that we're not. We can lie to him, telling him that we're doing great (like we're so prone to tell each other). Or we can admit that the answer is no. When we're honest, when we engage in a real conversation about where we are, Jesus will reveal who he is. And that changes everything. As theologian Oswald Chambers said, "When we have come to the end of ourselves, not in imagination but really, we are able to receive the Holy Spirit."

I don't need to love myself *more*. I don't need spa days or more manicures (although both would be lovely). I need Jesus, telling me which side of the boat I should put my net down from so I don't waste my time. I need to turn from my mistakes, tell him I love him, and follow when he says, *Let's go.*

I want to say to Oprah (and myself): *"Don't worry...God*

knows what you need... Seek Him first and all the things you'd worry about will be given to you... don't judge others... with the measure you use, it will be given to you... don't throw your pearls in front of pigs... ask, seek, knock... if you give good gifts to your children, how much more will your Father in heaven give good gifts to those who ask Him?"

Chapter 9

Getting a Sleigh to Fly

ONE DAY AS I was out in the yard with the dog, thinking about nothing in particular, I sensed God asking, *Trish, what would your life be like if you believed that I'll take care of everything you've prayed for? If you knew it would all work out?* I'd wondered about this very question in the months just after our wedding, thinking about how different my last two years of singleness might have been if I'd truly believed that God would answer my prayers and that my husband was on his way. I'd have been a lot less sad, I knew. And a lot less scared. Not to mention a lot less angry.

I tried to apply this approach now, to our current situation and my never-ending litany of prayers asking God to give us children. But I couldn't. Not really. Childbearing has a time limit marriage doesn't have. And whenever I tried to suspend my disbelief that God could overcome this, reminding myself of Abraham's wife Sarah giving birth in her old age, I'd see some TV show where a doctor told a woman five years younger than me how important it was to freeze her eggs now, because in five years, she'd have almost no chance of conceiving. That's when I'd realize that while yes, God *had* given Sarah a baby when she was in her nineties, He hadn't done anything along those lines in a very, very long time. Who was I to expect such a miracle?

I discovered something sad and new inside of me: for the first time, I couldn't imagine that God would come through. And yet at the same time, I couldn't picture what I'd do if He didn't. Just as once, I'd been unable to imagine a satisfying life if I never married, now I felt like I would always have a hole inside of me if I never became a mom. It would be a small hole. I'd be able to work around it. If Steve and I never had children, I knew we'd still cobble together some sort of interesting life: I'd write books, give talks, try to pass along good news where I could. And we'd have access to all the benefits of child-free living: romantic date nights, sleeping in on Saturday mornings, freedom to jet off to Italy on a whim (parents of toddlers loved to wax poetic about the freedom to jet off on a whim, I noticed; even the ones who weren't jet-setters to begin with). It's not the same, though. It would be just that: a cobbled-together, second choice life. We'd never send out a Christmas card with a picture on it, because what would we showcase, the new treads Steve installed on the back stairs? We'd never have that easy conversational fallback when we ran out of things to talk about. We'd spend our lives talking about other people's stories, trying not to take our pain out on friends who built lives contained by this room to which we'd been denied access. And when we died, that would be it. There would be no legacy, no proof that our lives amounted to anything. In Biblical terms, we'd have failed. I spoke to one woman wrestling with similar heartbreak—she'd been raised on a farm. "If I was a cow," she observed, "they'd have eaten me by now."

It broke my heart, it made me sick, it left me writhing in pain and fury every time the violent cramps set in for yet another period. I couldn't fathom how God could be so cruel. And as I looked around me at all my friends—the one grateful not to be born a cow, the many who still had no husband on their horizon, I grew more and more angry, wondering where was this God I'd read about in the Bible, the one who supposedly cared so much about His daughters. I wondered about Jesus' claim to have overcome the curse of Adam and Eve—where had he disappeared to?

I once heard someone define "sin" as anything that breaks relationship between us and other people, or us and God. On those terms, our childlessness was sin. I just couldn't figure out who to blame or what to do about it. *God is always good?* I said to myself one day. *What crap.* I read a book about negotiating hard times that said (with great authority) that "To the extent that the God we envision is less than all-loving, kind, and altogether on our side, we can't trust him with our whole being." *Well, yeah...* I thought. But the author didn't tell me how to get back to that shiny vision.

Over time, I numbed out. I nodded and smiled and attended one too many baby showers. I fought back—but just barely—the urge to kick a guy in his family jewels when he sauntered by me one Sunday at church as I was holding a friend's newborn and said, "It's about time you and Steve stopped being selfish and had a baby!"

When you numb out, I found, it happens across the board. I lost my ability to feel much of anything, which at times was kind of nice. But there was a sort of danger there, like I didn't trust myself not to blow up or shut down at any given moment. I stopped praying to conceive because I'd run out of words; everything had already been said. Acedia seemed like a vague old friend, something innocent that had made me feel a little down and perhaps prompted me to take more naps than usual. I'd have given a lot to feel down for no reason. Compared to feeling legitimately disappointed with how life was turning out, acedia had much to recommend it.

I developed a strategy to keep the fury at bay. When I felt myself brimming over, I'd go for a long drive. I'd listen to music by singer-songwriters like Michelle Branch and Patty Griffin, lyrics about loss and unrequited love. I'd think about how it felt, all those times when it was me left behind to pick up the pieces, and I'd cry for miles and miles. I'd focus my anger on the men from my past, lumping them into an amorphous blob, so I could stop being angry with God. By the end of the drive, the end of my playlist, there would be tears and snot and mascara everywhere—all over my hands, my arms, my shirt. I still wouldn't feel much—it was sort of a manufactured experience. But it was enough to get me by. I read Brooke Shields's memoir of postpartum depression, *Down Came the Rain*, and wondered, What do you call it when you feel this way because you *haven't* had a baby?

A friend invited me to a concert by Brooke Fraser. "You'll love her," she said, handing me the CD. "Start with the ninth song."

"Faithful," it was called. Lilting words about waiting for God when He seems far away flowed into my living room. She sang of reaching for what she hoped for—connection, tangible proof that God was real—from a place where the most reasonable response might be to give up and move on. And how, against all sense of the way these things usually go, this emptiness left her more, not less, confident that her faith in God is true. I wanted to feel that certain. So I worked with the little bits that I had.

I'd lost my faith that God was always good, but I still felt that God was always *right:* He knew what he was doing, that I didn't doubt. I read a novel about a child who was truly evil, who killed both her parents before she was out of her teens. I certainly didn't want that kid. But I still wondered why God couldn't give us a good child. I read Bible verses in a new light now, arguing back with Jesus when he said, *You have not because you ask not.* That simply wasn't true. Promises like "to those who are faithful with little, more will be given" vexed me now. Was it possible I was being punished for being a marginally attentive babysitter as a teen? Shouldn't keeping a dog alive for thirteen years count for something? My thoughts became ridiculous because the whole situation was ridiculous. The Bible—the place I went for comfort and guidance in tough moments like these—offered reassurance for every other affliction: conflict, rejection, sickness, death. Even martyrdom is met with an odd sort of hope that something more will come of it, that it's not the end of the story. But not barrenness. That's only ever bad.

A friend who didn't know about this internal drama (I think he just thought Steve and I were enjoying married sex too much to add kids to the mix) e-mailed me a video of

George Harrison singing "Here Comes the Sun," and my dam of self-containment burst. I so wanted to believe that George was right: that winter was over, that the ice was melting. I wanted the evil queen of Narnia banished back to the netherworld so that new life could grow. I wanted to believe it would be all right. I was tired—emotionally, psychologically. My hope, the little that was lift, was a slouchy kind of "I really do wish things were different" whine. Maybe my life doesn't matter? I thought for the first time ever. Maybe I was never supposed to leave a legacy? That thought threw me into that awful mental space of being unsure if life was worth the effort. I read interviews with author David Foster Wallace and his own struggle with finding the will to live, and thought I knew just how he felt. I went to church every week, a big sunny smile on my face. I'm a good actress when I try. I learned that it was easier to interact with people from a fake, happy place than to manage their discomfort when I was honest. So I smiled.

One Sunday, our pastor Brian gave a sermon about how amazing things happen in the presence of faith. *That word again*, I thought. I braced myself for another meditation on how God was only good. That's not where Brian went, though. He drew our attention to two passages from the Bible, looking at how this mysterious, elusive thing affects what God can do for us.

First, we looked at the oft-told story of a woman who had been bleeding for twelve years. Even though she was "ceremonially unclean" according to her people, when Jesus came to town she snuck through the crowd to get to him. "If I just touch his clothes, I will be healed," she thought. She did, and she was. She didn't get away unnoticed, though. Jesus felt power go out from him (have you ever noticed that when you're around an emotionally desperate person who is sure you can fix them, you can feel the strength leave your body? It reassures me to know that this happened to Jesus, too). Rather than scolding the woman, he blessed her, saying, *Daughter, your faith has healed you. Go in peace and be freed from your suffering.* After this, Jesus raised a little girl from the dead. This was, I suspect, a memorable day in that town.

Then he took his disciples to his hometown, presumably to relax for a bit and talk over all that had happened. On the Sabbath, he went to the synagogue to teach, and the folks from his hometown were amazed, but not in a good way. Have you ever dreamed of returning to the place you grew up to be hailed for your amazing accomplishments (like superstar country singer Toby Keith who wrote a whole song about this fantasy, asking the girls who blew him off in high school, "How Do You Like Me Now?"). This wasn't quite how it worked out for Jesus. Even as he taught in the synagogue with what everyone agreed was remarkable wisdom, all they could say was, "Who does this guy think he is?" They were offended, and their lack of faith prevented Jesus from doing miracles there. He was amazed by their lack of faith.

"What do you make of these two passages?" Brian asked when we'd finished reading. "They seem to paint a picture of how important faith is to God, as if in the presence of faith, Jesus has little choice about whether to act or not...whereas lack of faith limits his options, but in the opposite way."

Oh crap, I thought, the things I'd given up on running

through my mind. It wasn't as if I'd scorned Jesus like the people from his hometown. If he rang my doorbell, I'd at least invite him in and try to make him a snack. The problem was more that I'd have no idea what to say to him. I could see myself prattling on about the Patriots' chances in the next Super Bowl, or how it took five coats of paint to achieve the color of our dining room walls because the clerk at Home Depot gave us the wrong type of primer. The Son of God could show up at my house, and I'd have no idea what to ask him because I'd so lost touch with what I really wanted that my prayers were little more than polite requests that he bless this or that person, or fix the economy. Not exactly the bold, personal approach I saw people take in the Bible, moving heaven and earth to get to Jesus. They didn't make chitchat about sports or paint, they got right to the point: *Heal me, Help me, My daughter is dead — can you do something? My son is possessed by a demon — save him!*

I used to pray like that. God and I had had some knock-down wrestling matches over the whole husband question, especially after he told me to "take Jesus seriously," and then dropped me into a world that berated singles with, "You know, not everyone gets married . . . God doesn't *owe* you a husband . . ." I hadn't had my faith feet under me then enough to argue with them. But I'd argued plenty with God. I'm not sure what sustained my faith back then, but I identified with that bleeding woman: I'd had this unshakable sense that unless Jesus came through and connected me with the man I was supposed to be with, nothing in my life would work out; that if Jesus didn't fix things, they were going to stay broken forever. Getting pregnant was even more of a mystery. If God didn't make it happen, it wasn't going to happen. But I'd lost the will to argue.

It's challenging to maintain faith for hard things, especially in traditional Christian circles where people say strange things like, "Seek God's face, not His hand" (which means, as near as I can tell, "Don't treat God like a vending machine"), and sing songs like, "Lord, You're All I Need." Sometimes Christianity can seem an awful lot like Buddhism: don't want anything, don't ask for anything, and be willing to give away whatever you have at a moment's notice. It sounds so spiritual, but at the same time it's not very honest.

The truth is, most of us want stuff. Not so much expensive jeans and overpriced shoes (although I don't think God is against fashion) but stuff like relationships, children to make a family, a home to live in and a community to be part of, a car that starts every morning when we need to go somewhere, food for our family and for our dog. *Stuff.* I need God's face *and* his hand, and I don't see the dichotomy. For me, this "Lord you're all I need" idea isn't faith; it's the antithesis of faith. It's that evil monkey, swinging down to say "It hasn't happened yet, so that must mean the answer is no!"

No one in the Bible did this. Sure, we're told that one girl had Jesus over for dinner and just sat at his feet listening while her sister did all the cooking, but make no mistake: when their brother died, that same girl was right up in Jesus' face asking, "Why didn't you come sooner? Can't you do something?" Somewhere along the way, I'd lost my confidence to get up in God's face and ask, "Can't you do something?" I tuned back in to Brian's sermon, hoping to recapture some piece of what had slipped away.

"Now this faith we're talking about," he continued. "It's not agreement with some set of theological truths. It's a gut-level conviction that God can and will act." *A gut check*, I thought. *I can do that.* My mind wandered over the things I'd tossed up toward God over the past months: Our dream of having a baby. Our longing for a house with enough room for that baby, in a part of town where I wasn't afraid to walk the dog alone at night. Hope that my books would sell well. A job for Steve where he wasn't just providing for us, but using his gifts and passions. I checked my gut level conviction that God would act: *Nope*, it said. *Never gonna happen.*

I remembered a conversation—a disagreement, really—I'd had with a friend. "I'm tired of women being obsessed with marriage," she'd said. "They need to realize that Jesus provides all the love they're craving and go out and do something with their lives instead of just waiting around." She, of course, was married, speaking from the position (I'd guess) of missing those bygone days of freedom when there were fewer demands on her time. But I could tell by the black-and-white nature of her comments that she'd never thought of what her life would look like if she'd reached her mid-thirties or forties without her husband or children: what it would feel like to be the only source of financial support, or to make all her decisions—about health insurance, cable TV plans, whether to lock in the price of heating oil for next winter or take a chance the price would go down—alone. She hadn't thought through all the Friday and Saturday nights, the Christmases as the only single daughter/ sister/niece/cousin, not to mention New Year's Eves and Valentine's Days. Never once had she seen that pitying look of someone who was sure she'd never find love, so it was easy for her to say that marriage wasn't something single women should get worked up about, to demand that they get on with their lives. And she felt this so strongly, and was so certain of her position, that I backed down. This was, I realized, how I felt about the items on my prayer list: like I'd been fighting—with other people's doubts, with evil monkeys painting ugly pictures in my mind—and I wasn't convinced that the outcome would be worth the effort. I was tired of holding up the "God Can Do It!" banner on my own, waiting for someone (anyone) to agree with me. I wanted to set down my banner, crawl into bed, and sleep for the next twenty years.

Just as I started to get sucked under the quicksand of all these thoughts, Brian showed a clip from the movie *Elf*, about the effort it takes sometimes to generate faith. In the scene, Santa's sleigh won't fly because not enough people believe in him. There's a young woman who is determined to rally the troops and change this. She knows that singing is a great way to build faith, so she jumps from the middle of a crowd of Christmas shoppers and hops up on a decorative sleigh. After standing there for a minute, summoning her courage, she starts to sing—squeaking out a Christmas carol while the crowd stares. She's sure that if she starts, they'll all join in. Except they don't. They gawk at her like she's a roadside accident. She starts the second verse. By the third verse, you can see her flagging: this was not how things were supposed to go. And then one friend in the crowd, almost out of pity it seems, starts singing, too. The friend nudges her husband, who joins in. Slowly, in a scene that's agonizing to watch, the singing spreads. It's not quite what she expected, but still, something happens. We see the Santa "Belief-o-meter" inch up bit by bit as a news camera pans over the singing crowd, and television watchers from around the globe join in. And then, just as I'd convinced myself that Brian's point was the value of community sing-alongs rather than how faith can accomplish the impossible, there it is: Santa's sleigh zooms by, so low it takes people's hats off. It's not the cow jumping over the moon, but it's something. The faith of that one girl was the start of a much-needed miracle.

"It seems," Brian observed, "that the faithful choice is not necessarily the smart choice. Sometimes it's the more joyful choice with the bigger possibilities. It's looking at problems through a God lens, rather than at God through a problem lens." That, I realized, was something I could get excited about: looking at each dream I'd abandoned through the God lens and making some new decisions. Choosing the more joyful choice with the bigger possibilities. I read Psalm 119 over and over again, because the words of frustrated faith felt so much like my own. "How much longer do I have to wait?" I asked, begging the Lord to come through. The psalmist said, repeatedly, "I have put my hope in Your word," as if placing the onus squarely on God to come through on His promises. Was I brave enough to do that? I worried, fearing I'd make Jesus look bad if suddenly I became walking proof that not all important prayers are answered, that following him might not be all that good. I didn't want my next books to be about picking up the pieces when God doesn't come through. But in a few quiet moments, when I felt like I was sitting there with the author of Psalm 119, praying together, asking God to be God, I found hope stirring inside. I'm not sure where, or how. But there it was.

From this perspective, these lonely, fearful moments felt less like the end of the world, and more like Christmas Eve. They were excruciating. But also filled with the possibility the one who would save me was on His way. This made waiting—even as I stood alone on my fake sleigh warbling my determined songs of hope, wondering when this door would open—a little easier.

Chapter 10

Cocktail Parties

I TOOK THE T downtown one night to meet my friend Gwen for dinner. Walking through historic Faneuil Hall, I saw her standing in a small crowd, watching a group of earnest looking teens decked out in matching yellow T-shirts. They were dancing out a story that culminated with a guy being put on a cross, flopping down as if dead, and then rising again with some sort of cape on his back. He swooped around blessing people as the music faded out. Then the dancers pulled tiny Bibles from their back pockets and stared at the crowd hopefully, while their leader offered us the chance to be covered in Jesus' blood and saved from eternal damnation. "If you don't know the Lord," he intoned ominously, "you'll burn in hell forever..."

"They're from Texas," Gwen whispered, "near that place where the FBI raided that compound." I stifled a giggle as she pointed out that the teens were unwittingly lined up underneath a gay pride banner strung across the front of the building. I craned my neck to see if anyone was taking the teens up on their salvation offer. It looked like most people were slowly backing away. "I'm spiritual," a woman next to us said, "but I certainly don't want what they're selling."

It made me wonder, Did *I*?

The Texas teens tried—and mostly failed, from what I could see—to bridge a cultural chasm that was bigger than they anticipated. I'm pretty sure none of them were equipped for the conversation that would have ensued had one of the gay pride folks wandered by and wanted to chat. This seemed a shame. They weren't bad people: I spoke with a few of them afterwards, and their hearts were as sweet as their honeyed drawls. They cared about the people of New England in the only way they'd been taught: as an amorphous blob of humanity destined for hell unless this dance convinced us to change our ways. Here's the thing, though: We're not an amorphous blob. We're all in different places, spiritually speaking. Some of us are close to God, some of us are far away, and if the heavenly roll call was taken tonight, I bet there would be some huge surprises.

⁂

I've often thought that if I threw a cocktail party in Cambridge and announced that Jesus was the guest of honor, there's a good chance no one would come. Someone famously said that you can't mention God more than once at a Manhattan dinner party and expect to be invited back, and the same holds true here, with a few notable exceptions. Cambridge is a welcoming city, so long as you're sufficiently alternative in your approach to divinity to merit protection under the prevailing commitment to political correctness. So, you know, it's a certain *type* of welcoming. Spiritually, if you seek divine guidance from your bedroom slippers or the elm tree outside your office building, people in

Cambridge want to hear about it. More importantly, if you *dress* like someone who seeks divine guidance from their bedroom slippers or the elm tree outside their office building, you'll be a huge hit at parties, demonstrating the host's commitment to this open-minded approach to life.

Jesus, I've found, doesn't fit this "alternative spirituality" category for party-making fun. Saying you're into Jesus puts you somewhere just below members of the Rush Limbaugh fan club on the invitation list. (I live in the bluest of the blue states, remember.) And yet, when I'm invited for other reasons, he's often the number one thing people secretly want to talk about.

It comes up naturally enough, I guess, even when I try to hide it. People ask, "What do you do?" Steve works for a local biotech company, so that buys us some nod-and-smile time as I nurse my chocolate martini. The company headquarters is some sort of architectural marvel in terms of environmental greenness, so that adds another five or ten minutes to the small talk. But inevitably, someone will turn to me and ask, "So, what do *you* do?" staring expectantly, wondering if I'm one of those women who have their nails done, shop, then take the dog to the groomer and call it a busy day.

"I'm a writer," I say reluctantly.

This is typically met with thinly veiled looks of disdain; people in Cambridge are interested in tangible accomplishments, not vague affirmations by people who believe you can become a singer or a painter or a writer simply by declaring it so. "Oh?" someone will ask, with a slight note of pity, "What do you write?" I can see that they're waiting to hear about how my family always raves about my great holiday newsletters, or how I have a blog I hope might catch a publisher's eye.

"Her second book comes out next year," Steve usually interjects at this point. (He hates when people look at me like that.) This causes a most satisfying ruffle, prompting at least one person to blurt, "I've always wanted to write a novel/memoir/historical epic/travelogue—what are your books about?"

This is the $64,000 question. There's no way to field it without breaking the unspoken no-Jesus law, but at the same point, *they asked.* "They're about my search for spirituality," I begin warily. "The things I tried when I was looking for the right God...and the right guy."

"You found the right guy," someone will say, nudging Steve with a smile. "Does that mean you think you've found the right God?"

"Well, yes," I confess, knowing that saying I've found the "right" spiritual path is akin to taking the first step down the plank on a pirate ship. "Of all the things I tried—and I tried almost everything—only one brought any sort of results. It wasn't until I tried following Jesus that my life got any better." This is when half the group drains their wine glasses and dashes off for refills, while the rest of us make polite moving-on commentary, wishing each other well. And if that were the end of it, I'd have taken a job at an Ann Taylor store by now to get the discount on clothes and a different answer to these sorts of questions. But that isn't usually the end of it. In the aftermath of my confession, there is almost always at least one person who tracks me down later, at the buffet table or in the bathroom, to ask questions about my faith.

"Does it really work?"

"But you guys don't look like Christians..."

"Aren't you a Democrat?"

"Do you go to church *every* week?"

Some make sheepish comments about how they shouldn't have said that the canapés they brought to the party came out like *crap*, and that they hope I wasn't offended by their language. "Trish says stuff like that all the time," Steve reassures them. After a bit more small talk, people sometimes share bits of their own stories.

"My best friend became a Christian...I don't even know how to talk to her anymore."

"My cousin keeps sending me that *Purpose Driven Life* book. He says it will change my life, but it kind of pisses me off that he's so sure my life needs changing."

"Did Jesus really bring you your husband?" a woman without a wedding band asks.

"I'm pretty sure he didn't bring mine," says her married friend, whom I'd seen bickering earlier in the evening with her husband over the crappy canapés. And somewhere, in the midst of all of this, we get to the interesting stuff: What we believe, what we wonder about, what we hope for. We talk about Oprah Winfrey, and whether there's anything to *The Secret*. At least one woman other than me has had a creepy experience with a psychic, and someone has seen our church's ads on the subway and wonders if God is really okay with such a blatant marketing scheme. "Those ads cost money. How do you stand going to church if they're always asking you for money?"

In my better moments, I see beyond the surface of these comments and dive into what most of us really want to talk about: Is God real? And if so, is there something to the claim that Jesus is the way to connect with Him? Does following his ideas require us to abandon everything we enjoy in life? Or to shun our Buddhist/Atheist/Yogic friends?

"What if my brother is gay?" someone asks.

"Wait a minute," someone usually interrupts at this point. "If you're so into Jesus, why are you holding a martini? I thought Christians weren't allowed to drink?" That's when the conversation derails into a hodgepodge of assumptions about how good Christians have no fun. And I, someone who probably doesn't even qualify as a "Christian" under some of the tests issued by the keepers of that culture, am tongue-tied and awkward, trying to deflect accusations that have nothing to do with the faith I'm living, or the God I've found.

In moments like this, I wish that Jesus would show up and speak for himself, because I tend to be woefully inadequate when faced with the enormity of this task. I can talk about love and connect it to prayer and hope. But still it feels like I'm not conveying the whole story, like I just can't clear the giant Jesus hurdle.

Here's the thing: I'm pretty sure that if Jesus was at these parties (not to say that he isn't, in some sense, but if he was there in a form people could *see*, where we could check out his outfit and the appropriateness of his wearing sandals to a winter party, and comment on how he does/doesn't look like his most famous picture), it would be a long time before people asked him about the use of the word "crap," or the Biblical take on alcohol. In the Bible, when Jesus talked to people, he rarely led with "Wow, you've really blown it." Instead, he said things like, "The kingdom of God has come near. Repent and believe the good news!" as if offering the opportunity to step away from our baggage and believe that our dreams just might come true. Jesus said that he came to give us abundant life. That—to me at least—suggests that his good news has something to do with the dreams and goals each of us harbors in our heart...and almost nothing to do with policing our drinks or language. But somehow, that's hard to convey at a party where Jesus is, officially at least, not on the guest list.

Harvard theologian Harvey Cox talks convincingly about the impact of *story* in understanding each other, and how we live in a world where the defining characteristic of our lives is relationships—whom we connect with, whom we admire, whom we look to to shape our choices. Relationships are created by sharing our stories. These stories interact and influence each other; that's the stuff of life. Those Texas teens were trying to influence our stories without developing a relationship with us, either in the general sense (i.e., understanding enough about the city to know why that rainbow flag was flying) or individually. It doesn't work that way, at least not here.

The truth is, I haven't fared all that much better than the earnest Texas teens in my attempts to bridge this chasm. I'm often flummoxed by the pressure in larger Christian circles—magazines I read, blogs I see online, friends who live in more conservative states—to be constantly evangelical. I was tormented by Mel Gibson's blockbuster movie *The Passion of the Christ*—and I never even saw it. I couldn't fathom sitting through a two-hour torture film, even if it was God taking the beating. But I felt buffaloed by Christians on TV and online who insisted that to be a true follower of Jesus, not only did I have to watch this gruesome film, but I had to bring friends along to see it, then take them out for coffee and convince them to follow Christ. These postmortems would, the theory went, lead to a great harvest of newly saved souls. (The unspoken implication being that if the crop got rained out, it was all my fault.) Like so many other can't-miss sales pitches, though, in the end, I just couldn't do it. And as much as I sometimes feel like I should be going door to door, asking my dentist and hairdresser and newspaper delivery boy, "Do you know Jesus as YOUR Lord and Savior?" I also know life isn't a Dr Pepper commercial. In good faith, I can't go around singing, *I'm a Christian! She's a Christian! He's a Christian! They're both Christian! Wouldn't you like to be a Christian, too?* and insist that the masses be saved. Life quickly becomes untenable if the eternity of everyone I meet hangs in the balance between my profound belief in Jesus and my utter inability to explain that in less than 85,000 words.

∽⋙⋘∽

I had an interesting conversation one night with a girl named Angela. We'd met at the gym and decided to get together for dinner. She was a painter, but worked in public relations. We raised a toast to the benefits of finding a "pay the bills" job that allows you to pursue other artistic goals.

I was just getting to know Angela, but soon learned that she knew quite a bit about me. She told me that she'd seen a video of me on our church website and had been reading my blog over the past few months. She knew not only the names of my husband and my dog, but also the various details I'd chronicled about both of those relationships—how my husband cleaned up my spilled coffee and our dog loved to eat Kleenex. It felt a bit weird at first, and decidedly unbalanced. This is what happens when you put your story out there, I told myself. I guess I should get used to it.

As she told me about herself, our conversation got deep, fast. She shared a rather shocking chronology of the tough hits she'd taken in life — family betrayal, date rape, abandonment by people she'd trusted. She'd spent most of her life, she told me, feeling pretty much alone and unsure what would become of her.

"How do you handle that?" I asked, struggling to field such intense disclosure.

"Well," she said, "it's kind of a weird story. I was on my way to work one day, and suddenly, I heard this voice. *You're going to be okay*, it said. *You've got what it takes to meet whatever challenges you face*." Since that day, she said, this has been true for her in a way it hadn't before — as she faced challenges that sometimes felt like a series of high hurdles, she had what it took to clear them, one after another.

"Wow," I responded. "That's kind of wild. How do you feel about that?"

"In a way," she said, "life is better than it's ever been. I've survived some things that I never would have thought possible." Then her whole face fell, her eyes looking down at the floor. "At the same time," she continued slowly, "it's kind of awful. I mean — what was that voice? Was it God? And if it was, how does that explain the fact that I still spend most of my time alone, and I still have no idea what will happen or if my life will amount to anything, or even why I'm alive. I feel like life is this endless line of hurdles I have to clear. And sure, I'm making it over them now, but that still doesn't explain why I'm even alive? I'm just not sure it's worth the effort..." She looked destitute. I wondered what to say. We both took a long sip of wine.

Dinner arrived. We made small talk about the joys of Italian food, how many miles on the treadmill we'd have to run in the morning, and how the waiter seemed to be flirting with her. When the tension eased, I tried to offer the little bit of help I had. "You know," I said tentatively, "Jesus said stuff like that to people all the time in the Bible. Maybe you could find some answers there?"

"I don't need Jesus," she said, her head snapping up to look me directly in the eye. "I mean, it's not like I need to be *saved.*" Her eyes swam with anger, as if daring me to mention the pain and frustration she'd just spent an hour revealing, or suggest that some sort of salvation was *exactly* what she needed.

I thought of an essay by a guy who'd seen a giant rock on the side of a Midwestern highway, covered in runny spray-paint letters reminding him that *Jesus Saves.* He'd been embarrassed by the sign, he admitted, even though technically, he believed its message. I knew exactly what he meant. That day with Angela, *Jesus Saves* was pretty much the only hope I had to offer. But I was cowed by my embarrassment over things that had nothing to do with Jesus, things that muddy the water whenever his name comes up: snake-handling shysters who promise salvation in exchange for cash, the moral failure and financial excess of high-profile Christian leaders, the harsh judgment and political extremism so many of them espouse. I sat there with Angela, wondering if I was brave enough to disagree with her, to challenge her ideas about what the *Jesus Saves* promise does and doesn't entail. I'd long since realized that I can't hold it all together on my own. But it's another thing entirely to suggest this to someone else; to say that she might be just as pathetic as me, that she too might need a savior. Jesus' claim that he alone can fulfill this need inside us is obnoxious. And yet if it's true — if he's right — then he's the answer we're all looking for. I'm not always sure what to do with that. (In moments like this I often wonder why God couldn't have made me an Episcopalian, like Lauren Winner or Father Tim from the *At Home in Mitford* series. No one's afraid to discuss faith with Episcopalians . . .)

Over the next three days, Angela sent me no fewer than thirteen e-mails, paragraph after paragraph of her deepest hopes and fears and secrets. I didn't know what to say in response, or even how to conceptualize the sheer volume of information landing in my in-box. It felt like she was having this intense friendship with me, but without my participation. I tried to respond, tried to be encouraging. I invited her to a class called Seek I help out with, for people on the front end of exploring faith. I hoped that maybe if she met a group of people wrestling with similar questions, perhaps she wouldn't feel so alone, and wouldn't need to frontload every issue of her life on to people the first time she met them.

"Oh no," she replied. "I could never be in a room where people were talking about Jesus . . ."

The e-mails continued. I stalled, utterly unsure how to respond, or even if I dared. In one eerie moment, I understood why various guys had never called me again after I'd blurted out my whole life history to them on a first or second date. When I saw Angela's name in my in-box, I wanted to scream, "I'M JUST NOT THAT INTO YOU!"

I wondered how much pain she'd have to be in to get past

her assumptions about Jesus. Here was a girl having entire relationships in her head, without the people in question being part of them. That was incredibly sad. She had all of life's huge, unanswerable questions spread out in front of her, causing her so much pain that she blurted them out at whoever might listen. And yet when offered a low-demand place to sort things out, she balked, simply because I mentioned a name she didn't like. I wasn't sure what to do with that. The Apostle Paul said, "I am not ashamed of the Gospel, for it is the power of God for the salvation of everyone who believes." I wasn't ashamed, either. I just couldn't figure out what to say to someone who didn't want that kind of power. *Jesus Saves* was all I had to offer.

Chapter 11

Seek

THIS CLASS—SEEK—was (and is) the best place I've found to work out these tensions. It is a weekly "salon" of sorts for people exploring faith. We eat dinner, get to know each other, and then talk through our thoughts on this touchy, somewhat insulting idea that Jesus saves, and how one might think of that in light of the real pressures of everyday life.

In Seek, we work hard to ditch churchy language and examples of bad faith, hoping to shine a little light on both the hope and the mystery of Jesus' bold claims. We talk about the benefits of a team approach to exploring these questions, and how when we let Jesus dig down into our sometimes messy lives, he turns up things we might not expect to find there: things like courage and determination, awe and miracles, sorrow and revelation.

We talk about the Bible in the fourth week. After a brief overview of what the Bible is (1600 years of stories relating to God, with a surprising ability to speak to our circumstances in key moments) and what it isn't (a rule book of outdated principles we're expected to adhere to blindly), we spend some time poking around in an interesting passage where Jesus seems to be giving a lecture on basic agriculture principles to a bunch of farmers. We ask someone to read the passage aloud, and by the second or third sentence the rest of the class is usually glancing at their watches, wishing they were home watching reruns of *Law & Order*. But there's a line in the middle that always wakes everyone up a bit, where Jesus says to the few people who have bothered to hang around, *The secret of the kingdom of God has been given to you.* That gets people's attention. Here's the passage:

Jesus began to teach by the lake. The crowd that gathered around him was so large that he got into a boat and sat in it out on the lake, while all the people were along the shore at the water's edge. He taught them many things by parables, and in his teaching said, "Listen! A farmer went out to sow his seed. As he was scattering the seed, some fell along the path, and the birds came and ate it up. Some fell on rocky places, where it did not have much soil. It sprang up quickly, because the soil was shallow. But when the sun came up, the plants were scorched, and they withered because they had no root. Other seed fell among the thorns, which grew up and choked the plants, so that they did not bear grain. Still other seed fell on good soil. It came up, grew, and produced a crop, multiplying thirty, sixty, or even a hundred times." Then Jesus said, "He who has ears to hear, let him hear."

(This is typically when I look around the room to count how many eyes have glazed over.)

When Jesus was alone, the Twelve and the others around him asked him about the parables. He told them, "**The secret of the kingdom of God has been given to you.** But to those on the outside everything is said in parables so that, 'They may be ever seeing but never perceiving, and ever hearing but never understanding; otherwise they might turn and be forgiven!'" Then Jesus said to them, "Don't you understand this parable? **How then will you understand any parable?** The farmer sows the word. Some people are like seed along the path, where the word is sown. As soon as they hear it, Satan comes and takes away the word that was sown in them. Others, like seed sown on rocky places, hear the word and at once receive it with joy. But since they have no root, they last only a short time. When trouble or persecution comes because of the word, they quickly fall away. Still others, like seed sown among thorns, hear the word; but the worries of this life, the deceitfulness of wealth and the desires for other things come in and choke the word, making it unfruitful. Others, like seed thrown on good soil, hear the word, accept it, and produce a crop — thirty, sixty, or even a hundred times what was sown."

The key seems to be the question, "How then will you understand *any* parable?" Jesus implies that the people who stuck around, those willing to admit, "Um, I didn't get what you were talking about back there..." were the good soil, the ones who discovered the secret to the kingdom of God. The secret is that Jesus isn't giving us a rule book of advice on how to manage our gardens, but inviting us into a conversation.

That's what Seek is about, really—the conversation, rather than the results. Truth be told, the results are mixed. As with anything, it's easiest to focus on disappointments, to obsess about Melanie (who left class in tears the night we talked about evil) or Jared (who was last seen in a Harvard Square coffee shop reading a book by Christopher Hitchens) and decide that this sort of emotional investment in spiritual conversations doesn't work for me. Sometimes, I'm quite convinced that I don't have what it takes, that it's not worth the effort to bother. But that's a lie. It's totally worth the effort. Because for every Melanie or Jared, there are at least three people whose lives are changed by God, right there in front of my eyes.

There's Lynette, who came into Seek angry, defensive, and more than a bit scarred by her conservative Christian upbringing. She called me "Lord & Taylor Lady" behind my back for the first three weeks just because she didn't like my sweater. (It was not the loden green Ann Taylor, but you can imagine the impression I apparently made.) Today, Lynette is reconnected with her extended family, and chasing down dreams she hadn't thought possible. She and I are good friends, even though neither one of us has changed the way we dress. I'm not sure what happened... Other than Jesus. He happened.

There's Casey, who told our group in no uncertain terms, "Unless a Honeybaked Ham falls from the sky in front of me, I'm never buying into this Jesus thing." Of course, we prayed for a heavenly ham. I'm not sure if a ham ever fell (he admitted at one point that he'd been having odd experiences with falling food—some dinner rolls, a piece of fruit—so who knows what God has done since?) but Casey changed from a dude you wouldn't want to meet in a dark alley to a stand-up guy you'd trust with your kids. That seems worth noting.

And there's Deana, a Pilates instructor from my gym who cornered me after class one day. "You go to the Vineyard, don't you?" she asked. "I need to talk to you." She'd had a bad experience at our church, bumping into a guy who pressured her for sex. "I don't know much about the Bible," she told me, "but I'm damn sure that him diving into my pants falls outside the scope of *What Would Jesus Do?*" I invited her to Seek and was amazed as week after week, God answered her prayers: for admission to a graduate program, help for her brother, restoration for her family. It was like she discovered that she had a hotline to God, not just for herself, but for all of us. And as I saw God in these conversations, giving new shape to our lives right there in the middle of the mess and awe, I realized that I don't need carefully crafted answers I can hand out on leaflets about why Jesus is the reason for the season. I just want to be where this stuff is happening, and let Jesus speak for himself.

It makes me wonder: What if our cultural hang-ups about Jesus are all just smoke and mirrors? What if Jesus' claim to be the way, the truth, and the life are true? And what if that doesn't mean any of the dastardly, oppressive, or divisive things we think it might, but rather that God is saying to us (like a fine Italian grandmother), I've got a big table set here, and there's room for you. Come...sit...eat...?

As part of the class, we spend a whole Saturday together talking about the Holy Spirit. My pastor Dave shares his thought that while Jesus' rising from the dead is a key event in human history (the whole forgiveness of sins/promise of eternal life double-offer being a rather incomparable spiritual bonus plan), the turning point in our spiritual evolution is not that, but rather Pentecost.

At Pentecost, you may remember (or you may not—I certainly had no idea what Dave was talking about the first time I heard this), Jesus' followers were gathered in a room, waiting for a gift Jesus had promised—a power he'd called "the Holy Spirit" that would help them as they went about their lives. They hung out, they prayed, they cast lots to replace Judas. Then, in the midst of what sounds like an otherwise ordinary day, "tongues of fire" came to rest on each of them. They were "filled with the Holy Spirit," and even spoke in other languages. "Are these guys drunk?" onlookers asked skeptically. And then Peter, who up until that point had been the wacky next-door neighbor of the group—falling into the water or chopping off some guy's ear—stood up and gave the most eloquent speech of his life, declaring that this was the moment foretold by the Old Testament prophet Joel: God pouring out His Spirit on His people.

"What should we do?" the people asked, astonished.

"Repent and be baptized in the name of Jesus Christ for the forgiveness of your sins," Peter replied. "You will receive the gift of the Holy Spirit. The promise is for you and your children, and all who are far off—for all whom the Lord our God will call."

Peter and the rest of the Apostles (along with Paul, a brutal murderer who was struck by the Spirit on the road to Damascus and transformed into a key player in spreading the word that Jesus is the go-to guy in spiritual battles) spent the rest of their lives performing *miracles*: they healed the sick, raised the dead, cast demons out of people like the guy I saw on the corner the other day, staring off into space and muttering as he tugged at the belt holding his clothes together in the middle. Jesus promises that with the Holy Spirit, we who follow him will do greater things than he did; that what the Apostles saw was just the beginning.

This is what Dave means when he extols the benefits of Pentecost. "On that day," he argues, "everything changed. God came down to live with us." The power of God is in us, rather than off in some distant land of heaven (or Never Never Land, or our higher consciousness or true self or whatever else we might believe). Because of this, we're not like the people of the Old Testament times, waiting for God to speak to us through a once or twice in a generation prophet. We have Him living inside of us, guiding us, from the moment we decide to listen.

⧉

Our dog ruptured an anal gland. She spun and writhed and stared at us, her big brown eyes filled with anguish, like she'd sat on a mound of fire ants or the shards from a broken bottle. We rushed her to the nearest all-hours animal hospital. Five hours later, once we were back at home and Kylie was sleeping off her surgery, I called my parents. "We just spent $350 to upgrade Kylie's anus!" I said, trying to find the humor. I described the vet's horrid bedside manner, how he'd neglected to mention that the sedatives would render Kylie incontinent, and how now liquid ran straight through her—onto the car seat, the elevator floor, and her dog bed. "Steve just went out to buy *Odor-B-Gone*," I reported. "I told him to get the biggest bottle he can find."

"It's funny you mention the ER," my dad said when I paused. "Your mom checked into the hospital today, too..."

My mom has been on oxygen for the past ten years. There is a loud machine in the corner of the living room where a plastic plant used to be (begging for some poignant metaphor about how plastic plants mess with the intended cycle of oxygen production) and a long clear tube that my niece and nephew learned to follow when they played hide-and-seek with Grammy. When she leaves the house, a heavy (not to mention explosive) canister goes with her, ticking off the little shots of air that keep her up and running. Somehow, it isn't nearly as romantic as it sounded when actor Woody Harrelson talked about the O_2 bar he set up in his office so he could get high on life.

Back when Mom first got sick, I'd prayed the strangest prayer of my life: "God, please don't let them diagnose her." My mother is the most obedient person I know. If she'd been handed an official disease like lung cancer and a set life expectancy of say, six months, I knew she'd make every effort to wrap up living in five months and twenty-nine days just in case there was some sort of afterlife bonus system for dying on schedule.

So I asked God to heal her, to give her a life worth living and the ability to breathe, but not a diagnosis. He came through. The doctors decided she had COPD, the clinical definition for "We have no idea what is going on, or what will happen next." But they didn't give her a timetable, which meant she had no choice but to live.

But now she was back in the hospital.

My sister, Meg, called with an update: "Mom can't get air into her lungs, and her heart is failing. She's on morphine.

They're not sure what else to do." I felt the air leave my own lungs as I stared out the window at the house across the street: *Is she dying? Does she know? Will our car make it to Maine? I should dress warm; hospital waiting rooms are always cold. Mom will want a book to read. What should I bring her?*

I called Steve and while we were on the phone, another call beeped through and I took it, assuming it was Meg again with some forgotten detail. It was my friend Amy, calling about our dinner plans for that night. I filled her in, said I was leaving for Maine in an hour. "I'll pray for her," she promised. "Does she know Jesus?"

Does she know Jesus? Such a loaded question. The truth was, I had no idea where my mom stood in that particular relationship. In our family, it wasn't something we talked about. I was supposed to know. I think there's a list of Christian rules somewhere delineating our obligations to the people in our lives, and I'm pretty sure that knowing the precise status of their souls in terms of heavenly hierarchy is near the top of that list. The thing is, though, I've never found the how-to guide for this, the one where people describe in reasonable terms how to have this conversation without alienating everyone you love. I suspect these descriptions don't exist because these conversations don't exist. Think of the last time you tried to convince someone that they just had to try your new diet, or read the novel that changed your life: any takers?

I wasn't sure what my Christian obligation was in this situation. The Bible said to honor my father and mother. What did that mean? Was I supposed to rush to Mom's side and demand that she pray the sinner's prayer and give her life to Jesus? Or respect her wishes and let her be? I was haunted by the idea that her eternal destiny rested on my willingness to perform some sort of deathbed evangelism. I wasn't sure God wanted my last conversation with my wonderful Mother to take this tone. So I did the only thing I could think of: I prayed.

Five days later, they discharged Mom from the hospital. She wasn't better, but apparently if doctors can't figure out why you can't breathe, they send you home until you come up with a more cooperative way to be sick. Meg and I sat with Mom at her kitchen table, helping her fill out a hospital form the discharge nurse gave her to define her final wishes. It was printed on paper with a pink swirly design; it looked like something recycled from the maternity ward. It asked basic questions about Mom's medical history and current meds; we filled out the details of her *Do Not Resuscitate* order. I was certain this information was in her file already, but I went along, glad to have these few moments together. Once we made it past the basics, the form got kind of funny. "Do you have a special poem you'd like us to recite if you're unconscious?" Meg read with a smirk. I struggled to remember the lyrics to a salty Irish limerick. We're not really a deathbed poetry kind of family. "How about sacred music?" Meg asked next. "Or is there a dance you'd like performed?" I burst out laughing, imagining the look on the stodgy doctors' faces if Meg and I broke out into an impromptu *Swan Lake* recital around our comatose mother's deathbed, as if ushering her toward a big, happy flock in the sky. I couldn't imagine how any of this would matter to a dying patient struggling to breathe, but I'll say this: it gave us a fun moment in the midst of all that sadness.

"Jesus," I prayed that night, "what do you want me to do?" I assumed it was my *Christian duty* to put my relationship with my mother aside for the sake of her soul, to man-up (or woman-up, as the case may be) and bring her the tough-love reality of heaven and hell. In my heart, I was already asking her to forgive me for the respectful boundaries I was about to mow down.

That's when Jesus broke in, bringing his tough love instead: *How dare you assume to know my relationship with your parents?* he asked. *How do you know I'm not with them right now? How do you know they don't know me? Don't mess that up by charging into your mom's hospital room with theories you don't understand. Talk to me,* he said. *Ask me. Trust me to take care of your parents.*

That was five years ago. Mom rebounded after we filled out that form. I think the prospect of Meg's and my singing, dancing, and reciting sacred poetry forced her to live just to avoid the spectacle. Or perhaps it was the prayer, and Jesus' promise that he cares about my mom even more than I do. It's like somehow, he's been a guest at our party all along.

Chapter 12

You're Still Pro-Choice, Right?

"YOU'RE STILL PRO-CHOICE, RIGHT?" This question came, surprisingly, from the most dedicated Republican I knew. Sean considered himself a testimony to the veracity of Reaganomics, a proud beneficiary of the free market system, and a self-anointed standard bearer for the return to all that is right and true and good. (Between you and me, his vision for what this return might entail was culled from the many episodes of *Happy Days* he watched as a child, but his cheery view of what is possible in our country made him more fun to be around than folks who wouldn't stop talking about how we're going to hell in a handbasket.)

Since the moment we first met, Sean and I disagreed. I saw him as a quasi-Nazi conservative; he saw me as a spiritually wacky, airy-fairy flower child, the feminist liberal who wouldn't stop bugging him about why his maid and nanny didn't have health insurance. Somehow, though, our friendship worked.

Sean was baffled by my turn to Jesus. It was something he couldn't disagree with. As a card-carrying member of his own church's vestry, he was, ostensibly at least, into Jesus himself. But he'd be the first to admit that this didn't require him to *take Jesus seriously*, at least beyond the scope of his checkbook. That night, as we caught up and traded small talk at a mutual friend's art installation, I could almost feel him casting around for some perch from which to argue, some clear area where he could say without a doubt that I was *wrong* and he was *right*, so we could spend the next few minutes in the typical sparring pattern we'd always enjoyed.

"You're still pro-choice, right?" he asked, sure he'd found a ringer.

"I'm not sure how I feel about that," I admitted, staring down at a black splotch on the hardwood floor. "I'm still figuring it out."

Let me stop here and admit: It *had* occurred to me, when I first considered what it would mean to take Jesus seriously, that God might want a say in how I handled my politics. I thought he'd transform me into a Republican. That's what Christians *were*, I thought — it was part of the membership package, right along with Amy Grant songs from the 1980s and high hair. Given that this was no less impossible for me to imagine than the equally preposterous idea that I wouldn't have sex again until I got married, I said, "Sure! Bring it on!" I assumed that the transformation would happen supernaturally, that I'd wake up one morning and find myself nodding in agreement with the pundits on FOX News, infuriated that someone might interfere with my right to bear arms, longing to protect my earnings from any form of taxation. When this didn't happen, I attributed it to my lack of arms and earnings, rather than the possibility that God might have a more nuanced version of politics than His front men advocated. But it never happened. I waited, expectantly, for someone or something to throw the switch and send me reeling toward the Right; for the Bible to offer a different perspective on the beliefs I'd clung to about human rights, opportunity for those who lacked hope, for spreading the wealth around a bit so we could all enjoy the party (and by party, I meant "celebration of life's riches," rather than "political machine"). But Jesus spent so much time reminding his disciples to take care of widows and orphans and feed the poor, I could almost picture him walking around with a Carter/Mondale sticker on his robe. But then there was Paul the Apostle, who constantly said things straight off the Family Values platform. I wasn't sure what to make of this dichotomy.

As much as I'd wrestled with the abortion question since I started hanging out with Jesus, I couldn't fathom switching my stance to oppose choice, to suddenly agree that government restriction was okay. It wasn't — had never been — that I thought abortion was good. Abortion is a tragic attempt to resolve the myriad tensions of our society's burgeoning sexuality. But to deem it illegal felt like the proverbial hammer, always a poor choice when the precision of a scalpel is needed. To put it bluntly, the idea of our ever-changing government making life-or-death choices about my body scared me. I opposed it on the same grounds I opposed legalizing capital punishment: it seemed like a slippery slope, a bigger burden than our government could bear. And while I was pretty sure God wasn't going to tell me He was *for* abortion, I couldn't help but wonder if it wasn't a more nuanced issue than the usual terms of the conversation?

We women have lots of choices. I know this—I've exercised them. I've chosen not to have sex with some of the men I dated, and to have sex with others. I've chosen to use birth control in those cases. I've chosen to think about long-term consequences in terms only I understand, such as: How could I handle an abortion when I'm so squeamish about medical procedures that I get light-headed when the nurse comes in to take my blood pressure? How would I face being connected to a man—irrevocably, eternally—by a child, even if he and I ultimately decided that we hated each other? How would I fare in the shoes of my friend Sara, who took the pill but still ended up pregnant with twins, and was now married and living in her father's basement with a guy she was dating just for fun? Or my friend Maggie, stuck in Rhode Island for the next eighteen years because she shares custody with a one-night stand who obtained a court order that forbids her and their child from leaving the state?

I was, I realized, still *exceedingly* pro "choice." But I was exasperated that as women, we'd boiled choice down to the worst-case scenario, rather than insisting that our capacity to choose includes the ability to make smarter decisions earlier in the process. Because let's be honest: We have a whole host of options that can keep us out of the *Roe v. Wade* dilemma. Our "choices" begin way before a guy's hand is on the top button of our jeans. In my heart (and certainly my mind) I knew we could do better.

That night at the art party, after I'd waded awkwardly through my emerging thoughts on abortion, I knew what Sean would say next, before he even opened his mouth. "What about gay rights?" he asked, a giant Cheshire grin spreading across his face. "Are you denying your liberal roots and condemning your gay brothers and sisters to hell?"

"No," I responded, trying not to get defensive. I'd heard public Christians tossing around all manner of horrifying rhetoric about "The Gays": sweeping pronouncements about their alleged agenda, promiscuous lifestyles, and how Rosie O'Donnell was adopting all those orphan babies and really should be stopped. Aside from the fear and anger, I was always struck by how odd it was to hear such a wide swath of humanity lumped into a single group, as if the spiritual strengths and weaknesses of the chubby gay grandmas who lived across the street from me were the same as those of my twenty-something friend Rex (who burst out of the closet right after law school and took himself on a three-month hedonistic sex tour of Canada). Somehow, it was hard for me to think of them as having all that much in common.

I'd watched Rosie O'Donnell. She — like so many of us — was really funny when she wasn't being strident or mean. But as I watched her work out her politics and her anger on TV, one thing seemed crystal clear: If Jesus were a guest on *The View*, talking to Rosie, I don't think her sex life would come up for a long, long time. I bet he'd ask her about the loss of her mother when she was a little girl, and how she was doing with her depression. I think he'd have dinner with Rosie and her wife, Kelly, and all those kids, and then entertain them all afterwards by walking across the top of the pool. Eventually, sex would come up. It always does, for each of us, because it's a part of life. But I didn't think that's what Jesus thinks of first when he looks into Rosie's heart. I tried to explain all this to Sean.

As we were walking out of the party, I told a joke I'd heard by comedienne Lynn Lavner to try to lighten the mood. It was something about how the Bible contains six admonishments to homosexuals, and three hundred and sixty admonishments to heterosexuals. "That doesn't mean God doesn't like heterosexuals," I explained with a grin. "It's just that we need more supervision."

Sean looked at me and rolled his eyes.

After Steve and I were married, I couldn't get my paperwork lined up in time to vote in the 2004 presidential election. I was furious about this. A core part of my identity was being a good American, one who made my voice heard in the political process. (Were I the bumper sticker type, my car would no doubt have sported one of those caustic *Don't Vote? Don't Complain!* reminders that come out every four years.) But as I mentioned this to God, asking for a little divine intervention with the bureaucracy in my new home state, He had offered an unexpected perspective. *You're full of pride about your politics,* He said. *It doesn't serve you, and it doesn't help Me.*

I didn't know what He meant. "What do you want me to do?" I asked. "Surely you want me to vote?"

I don't want you to vote for a while, He said. *I want you to THINK. Consider a bigger picture. And pray.*

This was the start of a long lesson for me about navigating the messy intersection between faith and politics.

When my first book came out, my publicist scored invitations for me from all different media outlets, including a few Christian television programs. One show even sent a team out to our condo in Cambridge to film a segment about my unorthodox faith journey. The prospect of being on this show brought me face-to-face with how far outside Christian culture I still felt. I'd never been to a "Pot Blessing" dinner; I didn't grow up doing family devotionals around the dinner table; I didn't cringe when people swore unless they put a particularly creative twist on it. I spoke *Christianese* at about the same level as I spoke French: *je ne said what?* I understood most of what was said, but I didn't always know exactly what people meant, or how to make them understand me. ("What's your salvation date?" my publicist had asked before she sent them my information. "2002–2004," I'd replied. I don't think this was the answer they were looking for. I suspect, in fact, that the form my publicist had in front of her had three little boxes to fill in, delineating a single, specific month/day/year. I still don't know how she finagled my response.) I wasn't sure how to be *me* on a show so quintessentially them.

The filming process was fascinating. I had no idea how much work went into a single, three-minute piece. We shot "B-roll" footage of me around town — looking in the window of a New Age bookstore; riding the subway looking lost and forlorn; sitting on a bench staring off into space and contemplating my plight. Then we went back to the condo, where the crew did all manner of decorating tricks to create the perfect backdrop. They tried to film Steve and me cooking together in the kitchen, which was pitiful: I'd spent all my time frantically cleaning every surface of our house because TV cameras were coming; I hadn't been to the grocery store in weeks. We pulled an anemic piece of celery and a lone onion from the crisper, and sat at our kitchen table to chop and chat. (Have you ever noticed how many interview segments include a "chopping random food in the kitchen" shot?) Now, Steve and I learned long ago that I can't multitask, and (as it turns out) he can't even uni-task when it comes to chopping. He massacred that poor onion, hacking at it like it was an intruder threatening the safety of his family. We stopped when the whole crew was laughing so hard they couldn't speak. "Maybe we should film you reading the Bible together," the producer suggested. "I think something without knives would be better." We gamely got our Bibles and opened to Paul's first letter to the Corinthians. Steve and I have never, ever, sat down and done a Bible study together. But wow, can we fake it well.

Then the producer interviewed me, asking about my experiences with astrology, Feng Shui, *A Course in Miracles*, and the disastrous romances that accompanied those spiritual adventures. It went along fine for the most part, until the awkward moment when she asked, "How do your family and friends respond when you tell them you're a Christian?"

Without thinking, I blurted, "Oh, I never tell *anyone* I'm a Christian."

"Stop camera," she said, her hand flying up to block the lens. She looked as if I'd just revealed a secret career selling kidneys on the black market. "What do you mean, you don't consider yourself a Christian?" I could see her calculating weeks of work whirling down the drain.

"I didn't say that I don't consider myself a Christian," I corrected her carefully. "Just that I don't tell people that's what I am. I tell them I'm into Jesus." Over the next few minutes, I reassured her of my Christian credibility: "I have a favorite Bible verse, I believe Jesus died for my sins, I share my faith with others..." My mind spun as I tried to think of all the benchmarks Bible-Belters use to determine who's in and who's out. We'd had an entire conversation at lunch about the Holy Spirit; I was surprised how quickly doubts of my faithfulness could arise. "So you're *a Christian*," she said insistently, eyes boring into me as if daring me to lie.

"Well," I conceded, "if I lived in Texas, I'd probably call myself a Christian. But around here that term is loaded." I described how divisive Evangelicals and Fundamentalists had made things in the Northeast, how my family associated those terms solely with people who carry signs through our town that say *God Hates Fags* and vote against helping the poor. "I just tell people that I'm into following Jesus. I talk about how the Bible is the road map I use for life, how it's the best self-help book I've found." I'm not sure she believed me, but she let the cameras roll.

I tuned in on the designated airdate, wondering what I'd see. The producer had pulled together an inspiring piece, and the filming was beautiful. But it was jarring to see myself on a show so full of right-wing political pronouncements. The news section at the top of the hour was like a Republican Party info-mercial: They talked about the 2008 elections, suggesting that if Barack Obama won it would be because of a fringe group registering millions of deceased voters and we should demand a recount. After that came a feature on coal ("Not dangerous! Not a pollutant!") and a promise that we were kicking some serious Iraqi butt in the war on terror. I couldn't figure out how any of this was helpful on a show about Jesus. I felt strangely misrepresented, like I should have said somewhere in the interview that my view was different; that I didn't believe following Jesus came with an auto-enroll in the GOP.

Later, I read an interview with one of the Dixie Chicks, where she talked about their choice to go up against the country music establishment after the backlash from her band member's stinging public comment about President George W. Bush. "I'd rather have a smaller following of really cool people who get it, who will grow with us as we grow and are fans for life," she said. *Exactly*, I thought. It was hard for me to admit this allegiance. I find left-wing political blurts as hard to take as those coming from the right, and I didn't want that sense of *us against them* she described, given how strongly the Bible articulates the blessings available when God's people live in unity. (As if God Himself understands what a challenge that unity will be.) But at the same time, her words encapsulated my true longing: As an author, I want to have a readership of really cool people who get it, who believe that the life of faith is about adventure more than rules, who will allow me to grow and grow with me. They can believe whatever they want politically . . . so long as they don't presume to speak for Jesus (or his people).

So now, this is my political action plan: keep my mouth shut about the things that divide us, and pray about them instead. I ask God for the bigger picture, and sometimes I hear back. I don't know the answers to wartime questions, or why some places are hit by natural disasters again and again without respite. We live in a complicated, messy, intense spiritual world. But I know the feeling of joy that comes from sitting at a table of friends who have political beliefs all across the spectrum, and realizing that we agree on more than the pundits would have us believe. When I take the time to look—to ask real questions and dig beneath pat answers—I discover that our dreams about the world we'd like to inhabit are remarkably similar. I voted in this last election (God finally freed up the red tape), and I read the *New York Times* online more days than not. But I no longer believe that politics will take us where we want to go. To quote former Bush advisor David Kuo:

"For too long I've held this secret hope that just the right guy doing just the right thing would make America better: obliterate poverty, obviate the need for abortions, eliminate loneliness, end despair, wipe out crime, and increase opportunity. But these hopes were misplaced and unreasonable..."

That's what God was trying to tell me that day before the 2004 elections—that my hopes were misplaced. The Psalms warn, "Do not put your trust in princes, in mortal men who cannot save." When we despair, when we feel like hope is lost, the Bible encourages us (repeatedly), "Put your hope in God." That's what I decided to tell Sean, the next time I saw him.

⤛⁂⤜

In my book, I'd written about how little contact I'd had with Jesus or his people between the time I put down *Are You There God? It's Me, Margaret* in grade school and when I went hunting the New Age aisle at the bookstore for help when I was twenty-three. Other than a few awkward run-ins with apocalyptically inclined wing nuts, my teens and twenties were, I'd thought, pretty much Jesus-free. But after a swirl of Facebook connections, a class reunion, and almost a dozen random "I saw your book in the bookstore!" e-mails, I realized that this wasn't the case at all. Jesus—and evidence of this larger spiritual world—had been everywhere during those years. I just hadn't noticed.

In high school, for example: I dated a boy for over a year whose parents were charismatic Catholics. They prayed in tongues, laid hands on the sick and saw them healed, the whole shebang. I remember listening politely from the backseat of their car as they described watching a cancer tumor shrink from a girl's abdomen as they prayed. I also remember, now that I think of it, that they had the most obvious sexual chemistry of any parents I knew.

At this same time, two of my best friends were pastors' kids. We never talked about God, not even when Jenny invited me to spend a week in Florida with her parents and grandmother, and certainly not when Brett shared the details of the latest sexual trick his freshman girlfriend had introduced into their repertoire (and Brett's mother thought *I* was a bad influence on *him*...).

My freshman year of college, I roomed with the daughter of a Baptist preacher. Sophomore year, I was next door to a girl who played Amy Grant's "El Shaddai" on an endless loop. Junior year was relatively Jesus-free, and a complete disaster: I was down the hall from a guy who brought two pet snakes to school. (Snake man fed his boas with mice he bought at the pet store, sent out in boxes that said "Thank you for giving me a home.") My fiancé cheated on me, a friend was arrested on federal drug trafficking charges, and I developed a two-roll-a-day Tums habit to fend off the pangs of my new ulcer. But that was also the year that ended with me dancing the lead in our college dance company's staging of an incredible modern dance piece by a guest choreographer. The music? Depeche Mode's "Personal Jesus." I must have listened to that song hundreds, thousands of times, the pounding lyrics about finding "Someone to hear your prayers/someone to care." I never heard a thing.

In law school, one of my best friends was Christian. She was conflicted—she'd saved herself sexually while dating her boyfriend, only to have him burst defiantly out of the closet right before graduation. She had all kinds of guilt-ridden sex with the next guy she dated, using repentance as a form of birth control. (She's the only person I've ever known that to work for.) I went to church with her once, when we visited her hometown in New Hampshire. My main memory is the T-shirts: One showed flames, a cross, and some slogan about how I had A CHOICE to make. Another said, "I've been crucified with Christ."

Wow, I thought. *Bummer.*

By my third year of law school I was truly desperate, stretched whisper thin from my three years of fruitless effort to reach the life I dreamed of. I remember working with a guy named Andrew on a *Law Review* project. We were standing by the copy machine one day when he told me how he'd met his wife in college, at a Christian school in New England. The way he described her was captivating—he told me how hard he'd worked over the course of two years to win her affection. He wasn't bitter about this delay. In an odd way, it was as if it made his wife more valuable to him than if she'd said yes when they first met. What I didn't realize, as we stood there sharing our love life tales while the copy machine whirred, was that Andrew was sharing his story for a reason. He'd seen and heard enough of my romantic trials and errors (Villanova Law School was small; we all knew each other's heartaches) and was suggesting, I think, that Jesus could help me. I didn't rebuff his suggestion. I simply never heard it. I didn't think there was room at the

Jesus table for someone who voted and thought (and dated) like me.

I looked back at these encounters now, pondering the many times I'd heard one of my Jesus-ey friends describe a fabulous, deep conversation they'd just had with a friend or co-worker, some interaction that felt like it might be a breakthrough indicating that the person was considering faith. I wondered how many of these "fabulous, deep conversations" didn't mean anything at all on the other side, how many of these friends and co-workers would have been baffled by our conclusion that they were close to making some sort of faith decision? How many were just being polite, or making small talk, or having—in their view, at least—a completely different conversation?

In his book about what he'd learned from American political leaders, Chris Matthews made the provocative point that what most people want more than anything else is to be listened to. We respect people who listen to us, he said. We pledge our allegiance to them. We follow where they lead. Christians aren't known as the best listeners. To the contrary, we're widely—and accurately, in my experience—viewed as people who refuse to listen to anyone who doesn't agree with us completely about everything: faith, theology, politics, whether toilet paper should come out over or under the roll...

Jesus listened. People approached him with their stories: *My daughter is sick; I'm blind and can't see; I want to believe everything you're saying, but I'm not sure I do.* He responded to their needs.

Recognizing this dichotomy and seeing myself right in the middle of it prompted me to do some soul searching. I'm more of a pontificator than a listener (I'd argue most authors are); you don't have to look far to find any number of people I've taken a blunt "You need Jesus!" shot at, rather than asking what sort of help they might be looking for. I'm not proud of this. In a moment of true mortification over some of my own conversations, I asked Jesus to help me change. It all came down to a question: did I want to be helpful, or did I want to be right? It's not hard to be right: if I believe that the Bible is true, I am (theoretically, at least) entirely correct in saying, to every person I meet and from every platform I can climb up on: *You need Jesus!* But in very few cases will I be helpful. I'll be shooting baskets that never sink. Whether I go 0 for 10, or 0 for 1,000, my score will still be zero.

I want more. I want real faith conversations without political overtones, and without the haunting pressure that I'm supposed to change anybody's mind about anything. I want to listen, and offer help, and then trust Jesus to be, well...God.

Back in my New Age days, I tossed books and horoscopes and all manner of weird prognostications to everyone I knew, not caring whether they adopted my beliefs or eschewed them. I'd assumed that everyone would jump onto the spiritual bandwagon eventually, and never worried for a moment about how long that might take. My faith in God was huge back then. So I decided to have the same confidence in Jesus that I used to have in astrology and Feng Shui, to trust that he can capture everyone's attention and break through the walls that divide us. What he offers is amazing—better than anything else I've tried. But it only works if I let him do the heavy lifting.

Later, when I read John Steinbeck's epic story *East of Eden*, I thought back to my conversations with Sean. "Most of (our) vices," Steinbeck says, "are attempted shortcuts to love." That's true, at least for me: I don't like to stay in the lines, I long to rebel and figure out my own path, the one I'm sure will be a faster route to the attention I crave. It's not though. I suspect this is what Jesus would say to Rosie, and to Sean. It's what he keeps saying to me, over and over again, as I wander off on my tangents and shortcuts and he gently pulls me back.

Chapter 13

Settle?

I READ AN ARTICLE in the *Atlantic*, by a single mom named Lori Gottlieb. She whipped up a firestorm of controversy, suggesting that more women settle for Mr. Not Quite Right. She'd passed up chances at marriage in her twenties and thirties, she reported, moving from one male companion to another in search of the perfect fit. Her mother had lamented her perpetually single state, but she'd fended Mom off glibly, asking, "Do you really expect me to spend my life with a man who has never read Proust?"

She turned forty, and her imagined Mr. Perfect never came. She had a baby through in vitro fertilization, assuring herself that she'd resume her search for "him" once the baby was born. This is where her plan fell apart. She underestimated the work of motherhood, she said, how it would drain her — not just on the inside, but her outer appearance, too. At the time she wrote this essay, at the age of forty-three, she viewed her romantic prospects with nostalgic despair. She acknowledged that before, she had always been the one in the position to reject possible mates as unworthy; she'd assumed that the pecking order would remain constant. But the whole game changed. She's lost her ability to compete, she admitted sadly. She's no longer as pretty, or as energetic. She has a child she loves fiercely, which creates yet another hurdle a prospective love has to clear. And as she looks out over the horizon, she doesn't see anyone warming up to attempt the jump.

Her point in sharing this? To warn other women. *Settle*, she implored. Don't hold out for perfect companionship. If a decent guy comes along who will marry you, *marry him*. She argued that we need to swap our vision of marriage being a couple riding off into a romantic sunset for a more practical acknowledgment of what most couples have: "What I didn't realize when I decided, in my thirties, to break up with boyfriends I might otherwise have ended up marrying," she said, "is that...what makes for a good marriage isn't necessarily what makes for a good romantic relationship. Once you're married, it's not about whom you want to go on vacation with; it's about whom you want to run a household with. Marriage isn't a passion-fest," she warned. "It's more like a partnership formed to run a very small, mundane, and often boring nonprofit business." She'd give a lot for such a business partner, she admitted. It would be nice to share the load and not feel so alone.

The week this article came out, three different people—my pastor, my agent, and one of my single girlfriends—sent it to me, curious about my reaction. I think they expected me to be horrified. My agent imagined I'd dash off a rebuttal piece, refuting Gottlieb's pessimism with my characteristic, "anything can happen at any time!" view of life, admonishing women to hold out for better. That's what I expected of myself. But as I read Gottlieb's arguments, I realized she wasn't an angry failed feminist lashing out at chick-lit books and Disney movies. She seemed sane, rational, realistic—I could see her point. She had, I realized, run out of "anything could happen!" a few years back, and now was in the sad position of evaluating what might have been. Marriage, like most things, looks different when it's fading out of reach.

Other readers didn't see it this way, of course. They fired off vitriolic rebuttals, arguing against the limited options Gottlieb set out. "Women can be FINE on their own," they insisted angrily. "What about the value of a community of friends? Extended family? Haven't we learned that It Takes A Village?" They ignored the substance of her message—the feeling of having lost out on something central to life and needing a way to mourn it.

Closing out her essay, Gottlieb shared an interchange she'd had repeatedly, one I recognized from my own single days: "[M]arried friends say things like, 'Oh, you're so lucky, you don't have to negotiate with your husband about the cost of piano lessons,' or 'You're so lucky, you don't have anyone putting the kids in front of the TV and you can raise your son the way you want.' I'll even hear things like, 'You're so lucky, you don't have to have sex with someone you don't want to.' The list goes on, and each time, I say, 'Okay, if you're so unhappy, and if I'm so lucky, leave your husband! In fact, send him over here.' Not one person has taken me up on this offer."

I look to the Bible for guidance about most things, and romantic choices are at the top of my "most things" list. If there is one point the Good Book hits home, it's that we're not intended to do life alone. The centerpiece of not doing life alone, according to God's plan, seems to be marriage. The Bible opens with a marriage, and closes with a picture of divine nuptials between Jesus and his followers. The pages in between offer countless stories of God bringing men and women together in ways that range from practical to supernatural. But the goal is always the same: the buddy system. Life is safer, better, and more productive when we partner up. King Solomon, looking back over the course of his life and offering his enigmatic thoughts in that passage from the book of Ecclesiastes Steve and I were so fond of, agreed: "Two are better than one, because they have a good return on their work: If one falls down, his friend can help him up. But pity the man who falls and has no one to help him up! Also, if two lie down together, they will keep warm. But how can one keep warm alone? Though one may be overpowered, two can defend themselves. A cord of three strands is not easily broken."

Help getting up after a fall. Warm companionship at night. Joint efforts to defend house and home. These were the things Gottlieb longed for in her essay, things that had very little to do with someone being a perfectly suited partner who's read all the same books as you.

The Apostle Paul is one of the few figures in the New Testament specifically called to abstain from marriage in order to better serve God. And even though he's been elevated as the Patron Saint of Single Christians (you can imagine how shocked I was to discover, coming to Protestant life after a Catholic childhood, that folks on this side of the *Wittenburg Door* have their own fondness for saint worship?), that wasn't the message I saw when I read his writings. Paul's singleness wasn't a burden; he was *thrilled* to be freed from the obligation to marry. In a time when taking a wife and creating the next generation were the height of duty for a good Jewish man, Paul felt like a kid who'd been given a free pass to all-day recess when he received the call from God to remain single, and he wished others felt the same. It baffled him that we didn't. But I think his status was somewhat unique, as the larger message of the Bible points unequivocally toward God's creation of marriage as the optimal status in which most of us might spend our adult lives. This is, I think, part of the destiny God placed in each of our hearts. We crave connectedness: It's why we tune into television shows each week to see what will happen to our favorite characters; it's why we hook up weekend after weekend with guy after guy, hoping for some spark of recognition or realization between us, something that says, *You're the one.* We want to be part of something bigger than ourselves.

I thought back to one of my past dating relationships, just before I left my career in law to enroll in graduate school. The guy was great — romantic, fun, handsome. I told him I'd been thinking of applying to school in a different state, and his immediate response was, "You can't leave now — I just found you!" His vulnerability left me wide-eyed, as I didn't yet feel that way about him. (I would, eventually, but I didn't then.) I set the grad-school application aside, though, because that's what you do when you think you might have found *the one.* (And before you yell at me, let me point out: the application, and the school, were right there where I'd left them when this guy and I broke up. Schools stay put, but people rarely do.)

Here's what I see now, looking back over this experience: If this guy and I had married, I suspect we'd have a fine life.

We'd laugh some, and enjoy dinner parties with friends. We'd probably have a couple of cute kids, and a nice home in some Philadelphia suburb. I can't remember how he felt about dogs, but I'd lobby for one. And I'd probably win if I agreed to let him take yet another ski vacation with his buddies. We'd have our tensions; life wouldn't be perfect. But on the whole, we'd be just fine. And all of this — the laughter and the tensions — would be better than life alone. Unless...

Unless I obsessed over the ski vacations, over the lack of a dog, over the low-level ongoing war between us over whether we should force child #1 into tennis lessons in light of his budding genius, despite the fact that he hated this weekly obligation the way cavity-prone kids hate the dentist. Unless I gave too much thought to my husband's vacations, and his mention that he'd been down at the hot tub "with everybody" when I'd tried to reach him earlier. Unless I spent too much time pondering the myriad possibilities of "everybody." That sort of thing. Jealousy was my demon in those days, and so I suspect that the ski trips would have unraveled me over time, no matter how diligently I worked to keep myself sewn up. But still — almost always — it would have been a better life than what I'd have had on my own, unmarried, alone.

So for anyone who is not into Jesus, the Bible, the audacious promises God offers us about a supernaturally abundant life, I line up with Lori Gottlieb and say: *Settle*. Marry that man. Seal the deal, secure the partnership, embrace a life where you're building something bigger than yourself. Settle carefully, of course: watch a prospective partner like a hawk for signs of danger. But if he is, as so many men are, a decent sort of guy with life goals that more or less mirror yours, and he asks you to join him in creating a marital nonprofit for the purposes of creating and raising a family, I'd say, *Go for it.*

But if you are into Jesus, the Bible, and the audacious promises God offers us about a supernaturally abundant life, I'd say this: Settling is the single biggest threat to the dream God has placed in your heart, and succumbing to it will bring a gut-level disappointment and unhappiness words can hardly describe. For those who know The Promise, this knowledge changes things. As I said in my first book, it's like taking the red pill in *The Matrix:* once you've made the choice to know, you can't unknow. And the whole purpose of knowledge is to change things. Knowing what God created us for — the type of marriage He intends for us, the very genesis of the happily ever after fantasy — diminishes our capacity to live in the world of marriage as nonprofit partnership. Once you under-stand the design of this union — and how God designed our hearts — anything less than His best won't fit. Like a cheap suit you pick up at a discount, it will chafe and itch and leave you tugging and pulling at the fabric, because it wasn't made for you. God's marriage will fit like Cinderella's slipper. (How different would that story be if the prince had simply crammed the shoe on the first cute girl he met?)

When you know, the game of settling changes. The man who comes along to tempt you won't be a harmless frog. More likely, he'll be a snake. You can walk by a snake unharmed. But if you stop, if you engage him, that's when you're in trouble. Most snakes don't bite — that's too obvious. Instead, they en-velop you slowly, winding around and around in what feels like the warm security you've always dreamed of. Then they start to squeeze.

This is what happened to Eve. The snake spoke to her, and she could have walked away but she didn't. She was curious (or bored, or mad because Adam hadn't read Proust) and so she stooped down to hear what he had to offer. That was the end of Eve's happily ever after.

I watched this happen to my friend Janel. She met a froggish guy at a cocktail party at an art museum. He was older, and a little drunk. She wasn't interested. But a few days later, he asked a mutual friend for her phone number and called to ask her out. This small gesture made him so vastly different from the other men she knew—the Christian men, so many of them perfect husband material aside from the small detail of their refusal to pursue anyone—that she thought, "Perhaps I misjudged him..."

He was a nice snake at first. As I mentioned, coils feel an awful lot like hugs. He surrounded Janel with comfort as her family went through an unexpected crisis, and made her feel secure as friends moved away to get married, to pursue other jobs, to chase dreams that took them around the globe. She had big dreams too, but the snake said, "Don't worry about that right now... you're so *fragile*... there will be plenty of time for that later." And then he gave her another reassuring squeeze.

That was three years ago. Things have changed a bit. Janel has been spared the decision of whether or not to settle for this guy by the fact that he hasn't proposed. It turns out there's a wife in the picture, and she's not quite an ex. It's *complicated*. He still spends the night, still takes up most of her time. But he hasn't offered her the one thing she's looking for. She's gotten her hopes up as they've taken romantic vacations, or when he's alluded to "something big" on their horizon. But to a one, these hopes have been dashed, and she's stuck pretending not to care. She's secure in his grip, and most of the time, the subtle pressure feels better than what she imagines the formless horror of life alone to be like. But she's losing her ability to even imagine that.

I saw a TV show one night that bummed me out. It was one of those real estate shows, where a seasoned Realtor helps first-time buyers transition from living with Mom and Dad to paying for their own square footage. Usually, I love the low-stakes drama of watching other people make such huge decisions. But this particular episode left me feeling sad for reasons that had nothing to do with ugly bathrooms or lack of counter space in the kitchen.

The show featured a couple: a twenty-six-year-old guy who lived with his parents, and his almost-thirty girlfriend. She was a registered nurse, going to school at night for her master's degree; he had just spent eighteen months partying in Hawaii. He was out of money and back in their cold city, planning to work for the family construction business. He brought some viable skills to the table, but it was pretty clear that it was her cash that qualified this couple to be in the housing market at all.

They looked at three properties—one was just shy of being condemned (the guy loved this place; his girlfriend recoiled in horror as things fell down around them), one was small but move-in ready (she liked the idea of having him around to pay some attention to her; he was bored by the lack of projects), one was unmemorable aside from having lots of dark purple paint.

After the commercial break, we learned that "they" had chosen house #1. "I cried when he told me he picked this one," the girlfriend admitted. It was clear who controlled their relationship.

The show visited the couple six months later. The guy had done an amazing job of renovating—moving walls to open up the space, replacing linoleum floors with Brazilian hardwood, turning a disgusting bathroom into a spa-quality oasis. He'd made good on his promise to not leave his girlfriend living in a hovel forever. But that was the only promise he'd made. As the credits rolled, he said, with his best charming smile, "And the best part is that I get to wake up next to this beautiful face every morning." She blushed and beamed. Then the producer asked, "So, what's next for you two?" which erased both his confidence and her glow. She shook her head awkwardly, shrugging and pointing at him. He gave another big "Who—me?" smile and mumbled something about liking things just the way they were. It was sad.

Living together is not a commitment. Buying a house is not a commitment. Brazilian hardwood floors and a spa tub are not a commitment. While she was thinking "our future," he was thinking "resale value." There's a reason rap songs say things like, "Why commit when you're already hittin' it?" Crass, but true.

I'm pretty sure I know where this girl will be in a year or two. I've been her, to some degree, and I know women who have made this same mistake, equating sleeping arrangements with covenant. They're not the same thing. Someday, she'll leave him, either because he won't marry her and/or because he'll cheat. She won't get much of her investment back from the house; his lawyer will argue that his sweat equity is worth more than her down payment. And she'll walk away, wanting to put the whole debacle behind her. It will pretty much wipe out the first half of her thirties, and much of her childbearing prime. It makes me want to cry.

My friend Leah made this mistake. She's still living with the guy, still cooking gourmet dinners and decorating for the holidays when his family come to visit and overstay their welcome. It's been seven years. (And yes, I know we all look at these situations and think we'd *never* let that happen, but the years go by pretty quickly when you're hoping against hope your investment won't be in vain.) This is not the life God created his daughters for. It's not the abundant life that's available to us. But the temptation of some form of romantic commitment—living together, shared purchases—seems like so much more than it is when we're looking for signs that it will turn into everything we hope. But it's temptation that leaves us empty, in a house built on sand rather than on rock, the one that blows down with the first big storm. C.S. Lewis says: "If we consider...the staggering nature of the rewards promised in the gospels, it would seem that Our Lord finds our desires, not too strong, but too weak. We are half-hearted creatures, fooling around with drink and sex and ambition when infinite joy is offered us, like an ignorant child who wants to go on making mud pies in a slum because he cannot imagine what is meant by the offer of a holiday at the sea. We are far too easily pleased."

Think about fairy tales, and how they drive us toward this single point: there *is* a prince, and he *will* find you. The prince is Jesus. No one else will do; no one else can connect us to the full realm of happily ever after we dream of. The prevailing message of the Bible is "We all need a hero. We all need to be rescued. It's not too late..." Even now, on the other side of this promise, I feel like I am standing on the shoreline, trying to encourage other women that it's possible, that it's real. Again, it feels a bit like the fabled Avalon: that perhaps you have to believe it's possible before you can see it yourself.

And when Jesus brings your Mr. Right? You'll know he's the one because the slipper will fit, or his kiss will awaken you from a long, nightmarish sleep, or he'll know just how to rescue you from the high tower you've been trapped in. He'll be a man of true character: the more you get to know him, the more upstanding he'll be. He'll have a dream, a vision, a goal—and will be making tangible progress in that direction. He'll see you as essential to this dream. But (and this is important) you'll retain full mobility. Your arms won't be strapped down; there won't be pressure to remain still, dormant, compliant in a way that feels like giving up. You'll be free in a new way, buoyed by a lightness you didn't have before. Suddenly, the world will seem like a vast place to live and work and play, your dreams of contributing something wonderful to that landscape closer than they've ever been.

This is the real deal—the cord of three strands (you, your husband, Jesus) that is not easily broken by vacation choices or debates regarding Junior's tennis future. This is a marriage with access to supernatural power to make it work, because the Bible reveals over and over again that what God sets in motion, He goes to great lengths to finish. But there's a choice to be made, and we each have to make it. Choose well.

Chapter 14

Glimpses of Grace

WHEN STEVE AND I were house hunting, one of the places we looked at broke my heart. An old lady lived there alone, and I'd guess it had been her home since she moved in as a newlywed sometime back in the '40s or '50s. The stuff of a lifetime was crammed between those walls: antiques, pictures, years of sentimental knickknacks begging to be dusted. A cardigan sweater hung on a hook in the kitchen. My mom used to have one just like it, something to pull on in the evenings when the temperature dropped that she didn't mind if it got food on it when she made dinner. The woman must have been cold in her house—sheets of plastic covered every window. And I'd guess she spent most of her time alone. The house smelled—mold, mildew, a hint of some small rodent that had died behind one of the heavy pieces of furniture—the type of smells you don't notice when you're with them every day, when no one comes to visit to tell you that there's a problem. There were signs that this woman had hoped for visitors—a ping pong table out on the sunporch worn by the elements, an oddly placed hot tub just off the living room that had almost rotted through. I imagined her ordering these things, certain her grandchildren would love them and beg to visit. I hoped that they had, that these rooms were filled with happy memories for her. But it seemed like a lot to hope for.

Author Gretchen Rubin makes this important observation: "Everyone from ancient philosophers to contemporary researchers agrees that the KEY to happiness is strong ties to other people. We need close, long-term relationships, we need to be able to confide in others, we need to belong, we need to give and receive support. Studies show that if you have five or more friends with whom to discuss an important matter, you're far more likely to describe yourself as 'very happy.' If a midlife crisis hits," she says, "one of the most common complaints is the lack of true friends."

Today, I have more than five people I talk to about important matters. As Gretchen predicted, I'm pretty happy. But it was only a few years ago when my human contact landscape looked altogether different, when I could see a future playing out before me where I was that old woman living alone in a cold, mildew-ridden house. It's still close enough that it scares me. I shucked friends off like old husks as I migrated from place to place during my twenties, never imagining there wouldn't always be an endless supply. I kept in touch with Kristen after college, but no one else, and when I left law, I blew out of that city in a U-Haul determined never to return. I repeated this pattern with graduate school, several jobs, my first marriage. I was into my thirties before I realized that while it's good to know how to quit things, I was far too adept at quitting people, and that I'd need a strategy for dealing with my mistakes and disappointments if I ever hoped to keep a relationship for longer than it took for us to hurt one another's feelings.

Anyone looking for a study of the lies that lure and trap us into loneliness will find a treasure trove in the writings of Caroline Knapp. A columnist for a local paper here in Cambridge during her lifetime, Knapp also wrote memoirs about every feasible means of isolation: alcoholism, food addiction, a love for a pet that superceded her love of people. Her books line the shelves in my office, prompting me to think more than I might like to about my own escape mechanisms. I've run the gamut of mild addictions over the years, somehow dodging the ones that land you in the hospital (alcohol, anorexia, bulimia) only to land in more socially acceptable maladaptive behaviors. Reading Knapp's descriptions of her drinking—the empty bottles, the drunken midnight phone calls, the long hours spent staring at the wall in her living room sipping cheap white wine from a jug—and the lengths she went to to hide it, makes me think of how ugly my life can get when I'm on a shopping jag. I know the insanity she describes. I've snuck bags into the house, maxed out credit cards, lied and said, "Oh, I've had this purse forever..." in an attempt to hide my gluttony. During one dark phase when I was a lawyer, I took all of my credit cards (I think there were seven or eight of them) and froze them in a bowl of water in an attempt to stop myself from spending. I couldn't cut them up of course; everyone knows you need to have them available in case of emergency. Unfortunately, my definition of emergency was rather elastic. Shopping was the balm I used to soothe the things that hurt. During my first marriage, I honestly believed everything would be okay if we had a full set of Wedgwood china with which to entertain. That we had no friends did not occur to me, nor did the obvious fact that when you live with a violent man, adding an expensive collection of breakables is a bad idea.

My credit cards are paid off now, my habit under control. But some days, when I'm bored or frustrated, I feel that urge, the enervated certainty that things will be better if I can find just the right book on Amazon.com. I can get weird about food (we can't keep potato chips in the house because I'm incapable of resisting them), and online networking sites (some afternoons find me frantically looking at every blog and Twitter post I can find, as if there's some important party I'm missing). It's as if this bizarre fear tries to take over my perspective and cloud my ability to focus on my actual life. And when my perspective is clouded by a fear I won't get something I think I have to have, that's usually when I sin.

The Bible is a great strategy book for relationships, because it talks so candidly about sin. *You're going to screw up*, it says. *Here are some things you can do to fix it, and to avoid repeating your mistakes.* Most people (at least where I live) don't like talking about sin, because it's unpleasant and feels judgmental. *Live and let live* is the prevailing sentiment, which would be great if life worked that way. But as we live, we bump into people: we rear-end their cars; we hurt their feelings; we say things that get taken the wrong way. They do the same to us. It's messy out here. I once heard a pastor describe an unusual element he includes when he performs weddings. Making his hand into a fist, he places it between the couple. "You're going to have a problem with sin in your marriage," he says. "You need a plan to deal with it." I think this is true for all relationships.

Jesus helps. He's straightforward: *If you forgive men when*

they sin against you, your heavenly father will also forgive you.
I said earlier that sex is the glue that holds my marriage together, but I think it might be forgiveness. Or maybe forgiveness is like the primer the builders use on *This Old House* before they put down the adhesive that holds tile or stone; something that prepares the surface and helps the glue stick? I'm not sure. I'm not that handy. But the two are intertwined. Sin and forgiveness wend their way through every aspect of our lives, calling us to make decisions.

One of my favorite authors, Heather King, offers these wise words in her own memoir of finding faith, *Redeemed:* "Life is a series of small choices: the choice between moving toward yourself or toward other people, toward God...The movement away from self, no matter how small, has infinite effects." I triple highlighted her words, because I think she's onto something. As I wend my way through this crazy maze, I can feel God pulling me out of myself—my head, my analytical approach to life, my tendency to look to books for answers because they don't ask me to form my own opinion if I'm not ready—and toward other people. I'm not always good with other people. I try. But I mess up. And it's not that I think I'm unique in this fact, but rather that I hate to fail at things and so staying in my own little cocoon seems, sometimes, like the wisest course of action.

It's my friendships that help me find my way out of sin. I once heard a quote by a renowned atheist saying the one thing she envied about Jesus' people is our access to forgiveness: "I have no one to forgive me," she said. I hadn't always understood that forgiveness was so necessary. But as life progressed and my mistakes started piling up around me, forgiveness was quite a relief. Some people can access this forgiveness alone, perhaps, but I'm not one of them. Life is a team sport for me; I need friends. I need people to whom I can say, "Wow, I messed up," who will listen to my confession as I pray and then agree with Jesus that I'm forgiven. I also need their help to hold me accountable to Jesus' request that I go and sin no more, reminders when I'm veering off toward a ditch they've pulled me out of once or twice already.

Finding these friends has required an elusive blend of two things: openness and permission. I'm not open with everyone. I have friends with whom I'm transparent, who can see right into my darkest dark and my brightest light. But I have more friends who get a selected view, and that's the way we both prefer it. In the first group—the transparent one—I try to add one more element, to get close to Jesus' promise of abundant life: permission to tell me when they see me messing up. This has taken many forms, come up in many different ways (most of them painful, all of them necessary). Steve warns me to watch what I'm saying, to line my words up with what God says about what's possible, rather than what our circumstances might suggest about God. Dave and Grace remind me that there's momentum and spiritual power in premade decisions to show up, even when you don't feel like it. Aimee calls on my preoccupation with evil, Chris challenges me to pray for what I really want rather than against my worst-case scenario, Dominic tells me to stop doubting that God will use my gifts and dreams for something meaningful, and Kristina cuts me off whenever I start to talk about how hopeless everything is. They don't do this because they like it. They do this because they love me too much to stand idly by and watch me veer off track. I do my best to return the favor.

In the Bible we're told about a group of guys trying to get their paralyzed friend in front of Jesus so Jesus can heal him. They can't get into the house, so they go up on the roof, dig a hole, and lower their friend down. These are the kind of friends I need, and I think maybe we all do. We're not meant to do life alone.

At a recent gathering, Dominic prayed: "We come to you expecting, God. Show us what you have for us today." Hearing this made me wonder if perhaps this might be a key part of every spiritual attempt to connect with the living God: the idea of *expectation.* Here's what I've learned about spiritual expectations: They're reciprocal. We ask of God, and He asks of us. Not in the way we feed coins and bills into a vending machine in exchange for a soda, but rather in the nuanced interaction that creates relationship.

There's a song I like that talks about our tendency to settle: how God offers us a feast, yet we're content to sit in a dark corner nibbling on a rice cake, convinced that's all we deserve. *Be grateful for the rice cake,* the saying goes. *Not everyone gets a rice cake…*As if we have no business inquiring about the lavish spread of delicacies God has set out to draw us near. It's not that gratitude is wrong. It's just that it seems so misplaced in this context, almost sinful. As if we're determined to do things God's way but on our own terms. It's like we've built a fence around us to delineate what God will and will not do, and like crabs struggling to get out of a bucket, we pull down anyone with the temerity to climb the fence.

During the publicity tour for my first book, several interviewers tried to get me to agree with their pat assessment that what I'd really needed when I first walked into church, what I was really searching for, was *Jesus*, not a husband. My response didn't make them happy, because that's not how it was. Make no mistake: I was looking for a *husband*. And in that process I was lucky to have Jesus maneuver himself into a position where I couldn't ignore him. But I'd be lying if I said it happened any other way, or that I would have been okay if it had been just me and Jesus. I know I'm supposed to say that's the case, but it simply isn't true.

Sometimes when I read the Old Testament portions of the Bible — the ones in the first half of the book, about life with God before Jesus — I try to imagine what it must have been like to be a woman in that time. I don't get caught up in things like cleanliness laws about menstrual cycles, or even the bizarre system by which a widow would be passed along to her brother-in-law for care, feeding, and propagation of the species (although I imagine that such a system might prompt a girl to consider a boy's family VERY carefully before committing). Instead, what captivates me is the idea of living in a world where people can't hear from God.

I've had some interesting conversations with people responding to the place in my first memoir where I describe how God said to me, one day as I was driving down the street lamenting my single state: *I have more for you. I want you to want more for yourself. I have a husband for you, a family…everything you want. But you need to take Jesus seriously.*

"What do you mean, God *talked* to you?" is a frequent reaction. Sometimes it's said with eyes wide in wonder, other times with a furrowed brow. One woman came right out and said, "God's not going to talk to me is He? Because that would freak me out!" Fair enough. But this last response is unusual, if my book-tour conversations are any indication. Most of the people I spoke to—from tarot-card wielding urban singles to Catholic grandmothers in an Iowa suburb—seem to like the suggestion that God might speak to them.

Of course, the next question is always, *How do you know it's God?* The truth is, I don't. All I know is that Jesus promised us that after he ascended into heaven, he'd send his Holy Spirit: "When the Spirit of truth comes, he will guide you into all the truth...he will declare to you the things that are to come." This seems like a helpful resource when making life decisions. I think it taps into that sense we have that our instincts or gut reactions are worth paying attention to. Pre-Jesus, my internal compass was completely off-kilter, leading me from one disaster to the next. This promise suggested a way to recalibrate.

It's a mystery, not a science. I've seen websites purporting to outline the secret code for these sorts of things, offering to analyze dreams and visions by ascribing divine meaning to certain colors or numbers (or animals, or parts of the house...). I'm pretty sure God is more complicated than the little charts we come up with. Author Bill Johnson puts it well when he observes: "The walk of faith is to live according to the revelation we have received, in the midst of mysteries we can't explain." That's what I try to do. Stepping out—with care, of course, not in a rush—into the things I think God is calling me toward, trusting that He'll guide me along the way. The Psalms are filled with assurances that when we're on God's path, He lights it up so we can see, guards our steps so we don't trip, and steers us around snares that could trap us. Today (unlike Old Testament times when God sent a prophet once every generation or so to pull people back on track) the Holy Spirit is this guide, leading us out, around, over, and through challenges. The Holy Spirit is how we hear from God.

"Why doesn't God speak to me?" one skeptical guy asked. We were in a crowd, and I didn't know anything about his story. But an image came to mind that helped me answer.

"My friend Denise doesn't watch TV," I said. "She likes the idea of television—the open exchange of ideas in a free society—but not the reality of how it takes over her nights and weekends if she lets it. I asked her once if she's afraid she's missing anything, like up-to-the-minute knowledge of who's doing what to whom on the latest hot reality show. 'Not really,' she said. 'It's not like I'm denied anything—TV is there whenever I want it. It's just that for now, I don't think I want to tune in.'"

"What if," I continued, "God's voice is similar to how my friend Denise understands television? It's available—we always have access—but we don't always feel the urge to tune in?"

I've always talked to God; it's as natural to me as talking to my parents. He hasn't always talked back (and I suspect there were times when some other type of spiritual entity was fielding my calls). But I was trying to make a connection, and there was some hope I'd get through.

Before Jesus died, this was not how things worked. Regular people didn't hear from God. About once in every generation, there was a super-prophet who heard from God. And there were specific times each year when one of the priests would go before God with an offering to atone for the sins of his people, but the chances were so high that this would kill him that they literally tied a rope around his ankle before he entered the place where

God dwelled—a space behind a curtain called "The Holy of Holies"—so that if he dropped dead, they could pull his body out. I've never gone into any prayer where the stakes were quite that high.

In terms of hearing back, though, it was a rare thing, such that part of the chronology of the Bible goes from one prophet to the next, because these were the only signs people had of what God was doing or what He wanted from them. What's interesting about this (or incredibly redundant, depending on your perspective) is that after God told Moses to lead his people out of captivity in Egypt, across the desert, and into the promised land, and gave them the rules to live by, most of these once-in-a-generation conversations with God sounded pretty much the same:

> God: *My people are ignoring my laws and all I've done for them; they're headed for disaster. Tell them to repent.*
> Prophet: I told them; they ignored me.
> God: *Tell them again, with more emphasis. Mention the words "plague" and "famine" if you have to.*

This is followed by said plague and/or famine, after which God's people repent and rededicate themselves to God. Until they forget this whole ordeal (which usually takes about a generation) and God has to tap another prophet to stand up and suggest that blowing off God is a bad idea. The prophetic books will never be made into a movie, because it's just the same people, making the same mistakes, over and over and over again. (Although Jerry Bruckheimer could make something out of the book of Revelation, what with all the explosions.)

Yet even as I grow exasperated reading this, I try to put myself in the shoes (or sandals, miraculously constructed to never wear out in forty years of desert travel) of the women of this time, and imagine what it might have been like to be one of God's chosen people back when they were new at figuring out the finer points of what this meant. It seems almost impossible: wanting to please God, knowing that your life depends on making good choices, and yet having only a cumbersome set of rules to guide you. Some are easy to understand (don't steal, don't kill), but others are a little tougher to parse. (Say, for example, your sister has a baby. And you, while holding her baby, are overcome with your own longing for a baby. Are you coveting hers?) Meanwhile, the priests, in between death-defying trips into the Holy of Holies and days filled with bloody ritual sacrifice, are making up thousands of arcane sub-rules to clarify what God wants you to do. The problem is, though, some of their sub-rules contradict each other, such that soon it's impossible to follow them all. It's a harrowing way to live.

This is part of what changed when Jesus died on the cross. The distance everyone had suffered with, guessing at how to live and what God's rules meant, was caused by Adam and Eve eating the forbidden fruit in the Garden of Eden. (Walk up to a tree called "Knowledge of Good and Evil," grab an apple and take a bite: how do you think that's going to go?) That decision was the choice to do things their own way, rather than to live with the protection and connection God offered. Before that, Adam and Eve didn't wrestle to establish boundaries; they didn't have issues or need to work on their communication. They lived. But when you add evil in the mix, it means every choice — the words we speak, the way we drive, the look on our face when we say what we're thankful for at Thanksgiving dinner—has the potential to bring good or evil, life or death. We have more freedom than we know what to do with, but no access to God to sort that out. Adam and Eve left us in the worst of all possible worlds.

Jesus died to atone for that choice, and all the ones that followed. At the moment he breathed his last breath, the curtain hiding the Holy of Holies split in two. We could now approach God in a way that hadn't been possible since that day in the garden with the apple, and there was no need to tie a rope around our ankle. Instead, the door was flung open and we were all invited inside.

I take this for granted now, thinking I'm sure what I'll find when I approach God. I've grown quite accustomed to His yeses, the myriad prayers He's answered in ways that went, just as the scriptures promised they would, exceedingly and abundantly above all I could ask or imagine. The husband was, it turns out, only the tip of the iceberg. God has given me parking places, jeans that fit, restored friendships, a red V-neck sweater to replace the one I threw away in anger after some guy told me I looked like Gilligan...each answer bolstering my belief that God hears me and cares.

There's a television drama Steve likes to watch. I won't say which one, because I'm secretly hoping it will be off the air by the time you read this. The writing for the show is painful for me, in that none of the relationships seem real. But what bugs me most is that at least once in every episode, there's a scene where someone hurts someone else's feelings, and the wronged party flees the room/building/car, slamming the door behind her. The other person follows for a few steps, yelling (in a half-hearted, hopeless voice), "Wait…" Then he gives up and goes back inside. This kind of "Wait…" (the one followed by ellipses, rather than an exclamation point) usually means, "I know I just hurt you, but I don't care enough to chase you down to make it right." I hate this conceit. I've had it happen enough in real life, not always in such a dramatic, door-slamming fashion, but in terms of fruitlessly hoping someone cared enough to come to me and make it right when they didn't, that it stabs me with hurt and recognition each time. What does it take to be worth the effort?

This is not, I think, the kind of waiting God has for us. If you're waiting like this—for a guy who doesn't call, a parent who never expresses approval, a boss who doesn't notice your long hours—stop waiting. Get on with your life. But do it with God, because there will be new waiting to be done. It won't be easy, perhaps, but at least it will lead to something worthwhile, something where you'll say, "Oh, thank God I waited…" Hope isn't about sappy platitudes; you have to fight for it. If you feel like your world could use a little widening, or a dose of possibility, or some ideas for how to walk on water (or if you're simply curious about the view from the top of the fence) there might be something here for you. "Let us approach the throne of grace with confidence," the author of Hebrews suggests. I say, *Let's go.*

Chapter 15

One More Girl Who Got Stuffed in Some Jeans

A MONTH OR SO after the Boston Red Sox won the World Series for the first time in eighty-seven years, a reporter asked general manager Theo Epstein if he'd taken the fabled trophy home. "No way," Epstein replied. "I don't want to touch that thing—it's been passed around more than Paris Hilton." I couldn't imagine being Paris Hilton in any context, really. But this random shot, out of left field so to speak, had to burn. To whatever extent I'd bought into the lie that men are fine with sexually liberated women (and I'm not sure I ever did) this comment disabused me of this notion. I didn't say this because I was a Christian, flying my shiny moral banner. I said this because I was a woman, looking at a relational world that seemed insane. Based on results, I thought it might behoove us to reconsider our strategy.

One of the unexpected side effects of publishing my book of romantic mishaps was that I became a go-to person for women seeking advice on negotiating their own complicated quests for love. I understood the impulse—I'd gone so far as to take a job with a favorite author after responding to her book; I even took up residence in her guest room. Acutely aware of how bereft I'd felt after discovering that my heroine's real life was entirely different from the life she espoused, I worried about letting these women down — and making Jesus look bad in the process. It was a strange sort of pressure. At the same time, though, I wanted to do something to cheer women on and help them out of life's romantic potholes, sort of a sisterhood of encouragement. It seemed like something we needed.

One weekend, I saw the much-anticipated movie adaptation of the book, *He's Just Not That Into You*. I'd joked for years that reading those wise words (and hearing them said, loudly and without hesitation) in my twenties might have saved me a decade of dating hell, but I left the movie feeling like I'd been run over by a tractor. Is it possible for art to be too real? Because this hit way too close to home for me as I watched one character obsess over a guy who barely knew her name, another trash her relationship begging for a diamond, while a third wrecked her marriage because it seemed more important to decorate the perfect town house. It was like the worst of our female weaknesses were all out there on display, mediated only by the unexpected (and unbelievable) goodness of the guy who stars in Mac commercials for Apple computers. One *Detroit News* reviewer (a guy) gave the movie a C-, saying, "The saddest thing about this film... is that it continues the trend of supposed chick flicks that treat women as complete morons. Ladies, you're better than this." I appreciate the thought, but I think he's wrong. I wish we were better than that, but I don't think we are. Underneath our many-layered facades of independence and togetherness, most of us have an insatiable longing: for the phone to ring, the guy to call, the big kiss to come before the final credits roll. (And somehow this longing translates to unattractive, non-sexual hobbies like scrapbooking and decoupage once we're finally married.) What made the book such a hit was that it called us on our despair, the insidious ways we lie to ourselves and to each other about guys: who they are, what they want. Terrified that we'll be single forever, we are that desperate, no matter how many politically-correct and evolved men might like to believe otherwise.

When I was in law school, I had a friend named Doug who regularly (and by this I mean several times a week) met girls at bars who were willing to service him in the backseat of his car. These girls gave everything for nothing; I don't think they ever even asked him to buy them a beer. I used to joke with him about standing outside in the parking lot to interview the girls on their way out, because I couldn't understand what the attraction was, why anyone would find it fun or sexy to go down on a complete stranger with no hope of reciprocity? It seemed like as women, we'd bought into a definition of sexual power that rendered us unpaid hookers. But I didn't know that for sure. Maybe they liked it? Maybe it was some sort of rush for them? Maybe I *was* a prude, and I was missing out on the thrill of a lifetime? All I knew was that Doug would call *me* the next day to make some sort of plans, and if asked, he'd have no idea what that girl's name was or where he'd left her number.

My vantage point as Doug's friend kept me out of a lot of hookups, a lot of dead ends, a lot of awful moments of being just one more girl stuffed in some jeans (to quote a song by Patty Griffin). I had the benefit of a different perspective, knowing for sure that those guys don't ever call you, because I was friends with one of those guys. And—more importantly, perhaps—I'd seen firsthand that when Doug wanted to reach someone, he knew how to find a phone. This was my first step in realizing that if you want a guy to do something (call, commit, propose), giving him sex first is pretty much the *worst* possible way to motivate him.

❧

I was hanging out with a group of girlfriends from church, talking about this chasm between what we want and what we do, how to negotiate the huge gap between what the Bible promises and what the real world offers. "So I was in the parking lot at Whole Foods the other night, sitting in my car," my friend Jaime said. "A cute guy walked by, and I asked God, 'Come on—is all sex before marriage really off limits?' I looked up, and the door caught my eye. It had a big sign on it that said 'IN.' Only someone had been by with a can of spray paint, and so on this one door what I see is, 'SIN.' I was like, 'Okay God—I get it!'"

Her story broke the tension in the room, and the false belief that we had to talk about serious subjects in serious ways. My friends were hopeful, not yet married, new to exploring faith in Jesus and trying to figure out what this meant for their sex lives. It felt like we were in the middle of a giant knot together, trying to untangle romantic dreams from what we'd been told about sexuality, looking to distinguish the false threads that went nowhere from the ones worth following. We'd all had sex before marriage, before trying this Jesus-ey faith, so in some ways this was a different conversation than if we'd been in Dallas or Tulsa, a room full of girls who'd pledged our purity to Jesus and needed to pretend we'd followed through. Instead, we talked about what to do with what we knew: that sex outside of marriage can feel really, really good when you're doing it, and (contrary to what some people claim), it doesn't necessarily feel really, really bad when you're through. We agreed, I think, that meaningless hookups can leave you scratched and dented; we were all past the point of fighting for that. But we were fighting for something.

Sitting there, struggling to name it, the best I could come up with was the right not to miss out. The stakes are so high in the husband hunt, and the chances seem so great that you'll miss him; the possibility of adding even one more obstacle to the path to true love feels akin to accepting defeat. The prevailing wisdom says if a girl won't have sex with a man, how (why?) would he ever pick her? It sounds like the stupidest choice she could make. Of course, the prospect of a guy who only wants you for sex, one who lacks sufficient self-control to wait or work to win your affections isn't the romantic ideal. But things are so far from the romantic ideal already that this seems a silly point to cling to. If it's true what everyone says—that men need sex/ have to have it/think about almost nothing else all day—why on earth would any one of them waste time with a girl who says no to the primary driving force in his life? It seems crazy to suggest we can and should resist the things that compel us, even when we want to.

And yet, that's what God suggests.

I told them about a girl I remembered from a TV show a few years back called *The Real World*. Her name was Genesis. She was beautiful, and tormented. I loved watching her ups and downs play out through each episode, even when she was making a fool of herself, because she encapsulated so much of what I felt. She had these gigantic, untenable hopes and dreams and talents, and a fathomless, untapped capacity for love. It was like she was waiting for someone else's love to uncork her. She was ecstatic and lovely and miserable, all at the same time (often in the same conversation). It was so hard to watch, knowing in that outside viewer's way that the choices she was making wouldn't take her where she wanted to go. It was like watching a wreck in slow motion. And yet something about her—Hope? Resilience? The stubborn determination with which she put her head down and kept on going, even though it was *so* cold in Boston that winter?—made me dream of naming a daughter after her one day, to capture that certainty that despite everything that happens, there is still room and time to start over; we can each have our own new beginning.

If I'd known then what happened in the original story of Genesis—the Garden of Eden, that damned snake—I would have seen what a perfect example she was of all that complexity. It's a story we'd all heard—the one about Adam and Eve, and how approximately fifteen minutes after God custom made them for each other and gave them the most lavish piece of real estate on which to make some love and build a life, they did the one thing He'd asked them not to do. My friends and I went back now, together, and read that story:

It starts out in a straightforward narrative: "In the middle of the garden were the tree of life and the tree of the knowledge of good and evil... The Lord commanded the man: 'You are free to eat from any tree in the garden; but you must not eat from the tree of the knowledge of good and evil, for when you eat of it you will surely die.'"

Pretty clear, right?

"The man and his wife were both naked, and they felt no shame." An ideal, happy world. Then along came the snake. The snake represents temptation, the possibilities that lure us away from God's plan for our lives. The snake represents Satan, and spiritual evil, and every bad choice we'll ever face. "Now the serpent was more crafty than any of the wild animals the Lord had made," we're told. "He said to the woman, 'Did God really say, You must not eat from any tree in the garden?'" (Note how he twists things, suggesting that God had implied some impossible, unreasonable standard, when all He'd asked was that they not eat from ONE tree.) Then we see that Eve can't recall what it is they are or aren't supposed to do, because she says to the serpent, "We may eat fruit from the trees in the garden, but God did say, 'You must not eat fruit from the tree that is in the middle of the garden, and you must not touch it, or you will die.'"

"'You will not surely die,' the serpent said to the woman." (Note: the serpent *lies*.) "For God knows that when you eat of it your eyes will be opened, and you will be like God, knowing good and evil." He suggests this like it's a good thing.

We knew what happened next: Eve took the fruit and ate it, and then handed some to Adam who took a few bites himself. Then "the eyes of both of them were opened, and they realized they were naked; so they sewed fig leaves together and made coverings for themselves." It makes sense when you think about it in hindsight: how could the knowledge of good and evil be better than knowing only good? Later, when God questioned them about their choices, Adam blamed Eve, Eve blamed the snake, and God explained the consequences they would face: Adam (and the men who came after him) would struggle to find work, to support himself, to make his efforts amount to anything worthwhile. Eve (and the women of subsequent generations) would have pain bearing children. And—in what I think is the crux of our whole, "He's Just Not That Into You" dilemma—God told Eve, "Your desire will be for your husband, and he will rule over you." Then God kicked them out of the garden, essentially saying, "The honeymoon is over."

"This," I said, "is our problem. Since that first snake/fruit tree incident, and that one bad choice, we're all born with a longing inside of us, a desire that cannot be fulfilled here on earth. This idea that the right guy will satiate this longing rules us, whether we admit it or not. It leads us into terrible choices and desperate measures as we try to assuage this desire. But even if we get some guy to marry us, this desire won't abate. More often than not, we find ourselves tied in knots about his refusal to be the man we think he should be/could be/would be if things were somehow different. This is when we start subscribing to decorating magazines and spending long hours watching HGTV..."

"Yikes," JulieAnna said. "That's grim."

"The cool thing is, though," I reminded them, "this isn't the end of the story." We talked about how, when Jesus came along, he offered an alternative. You've probably heard the passage from John 3:16: "For God so loved the world that he gave his only Son that whoever believes in him shall not perish but have eternal life." Jesus invites us back into the Garden, back into a life where evil doesn't rule us. In a romantic sense, it means that we don't have to be controlled by our desire for our husband—we can trust God rather than being panicked and frantic. But we have to choose to believe.

My friends and I looked at the Bible, trying to decipher what it said about relationships and sex and what it means to be a woman, and then the more complicated question of what that meant for each of us. Because if God is personal—if He created us uniquely for some sort of divine purpose—it stands to reason that our understanding of His expectations will come to us in unique ways, that light will shine on different areas of our lives at special, distinct moments. Our job is to pay attention.

Jaime's story of seeing that graffiti'd sign at Whole Foods reassured us of this, but it had its tensions. It left her in the gap space between what she wanted—a clear communication from God on this volatile subject, something that felt personal, rather than just an institutional rule—and what she got—a confirmation that this personal God raised the bar for her, both in terms of what was possible and what was expected in return.

Theoretically, I love the idea of high expectations. I've done great work in jobs where the expectations were high and well delineated; I've floundered painfully when things were left amorphous and vague. But the reality of high expectations is that they leave you facing a tough bar to clear. They demand something of you. And I'm not sure why, but as I passed from adolescence into adulthood, my capacity for embracing these sorts of challenges felt diminished. I say "felt" diminished, because it didn't make any sense that it actually was. My feelings were often illusory, red herrings that led me down paths of frustration and madness. And at some basic level, I didn't want to be diminished. If my years of heartbreak and missteps counted for anything, it should be an increased ability to rise to the challenge.

That was what I told my girlfriends when it was my turn to speak. They'd voiced all manner of wonder and impossibility about the idea of moving sex to the far side of the altar. We'd talked about logistical questions of self-control, and practical questions like, "Where do you find a guy who would sign on for such a unique way to date?" In the end, though, right before we wrapped up the cake we'd been eating and headed out into the cold night to go home, I told them the truth: without supernatural help, we have no hope of rising to this challenge, or finding anything worthwhile if we do. It sounded so trite, I could barely eke it out: "To pull this off, we need Jesus."

To their credit, my friends didn't roll their eyes.

"What do you mean by that?" Carrie asked. They'd all been baptized recently, and were sold on the idea our church had pitched about how "Jesus Empowers Impossibly Great Lives." But no one had filled in the specifics of this promise for them, and they were skeptical. Their lives had each taken a nice turn for the better, but were still shy of impossibly great.

"Remember how we talked a few weeks ago, about how right before he ascended into heaven, Jesus told his followers to hang out where they were until they received the Holy Spirit?" I asked. They all nodded. "Following Jesus has benefits," I explained. "The Holy Spirit—God, living in us. But he doesn't barge in uninvited." I struggled to find words for what I'd seen. How, as hokey as it sounds to pray, "Jesus, come live in my heart," there's some truth to it. It's part of the mystery, I guess, but I didn't think I was the only one to experience how that prayer changed things, how the Holy Spirit set up shop—almost like Julie Andrews's nanny character in *The Sound of Music*—and brought about new order, a new way of looking at life, new possibilities. He breaks us out of our everyday lives and guides us, gives us wisdom, tells us things we couldn't know any other way. And he changes us, for the better, supernaturally. He changed me, gave me self-control where before I didn't have it, made impossible things possible. He'd opened my eyes to the excitement of what might be on the other side of that high bar.

A few days after our meeting, I read a new series in the Modern Love section of the *New York Times*, and all my Julie Andrews-esque hope for my friends came crashing down around me. The *Times* had run a pre–Valentine's Day essay contest, asking college students from across the country to dish on what love looks like from their vantage point. "We weren't sure what to expect," the editors admitted, "but we thought we wouldn't receive many essays about red roses and white tablecloths." Indeed, they didn't.

The winning essay was fabulous, and heartbreaking. Entitled, "Want to Be My Boyfriend? Please Define," Marlboro College junior Marguerite Fields described a conversation she had with a guy friend about his relationship with his long-term girlfriend: "'The main thing,' he said, 'is I don't mind if she sleeps with other people. I mean, she's not my property, right?...I don't want her to be mine, and I don't want to be anybody's.'" In contrast to this friend, the author admitted that through her own multitudinous dating adventures, what she'd been seeking was some sense of permanence. "Sometimes I don't like [the guys]," she admitted, "or am scared of them, and a lot of times I'm just bored by them. But my fear or dislike or boredom never seems to diminish my underlying desire for a guy to stay, or at least to say he is going to stay, for a very long time. And even when I don't want him to stay," she continued, "...I still want to believe that two people can meet and like each other well enough to stay together exclusively, without the introduction of some 1960s rhetoric about free love."

As I read, I wondered if perhaps Fields won this contest because out of the 1,200 entries, she was the only one to admit that she wanted things to be different. It takes a crazy sort of courage to fend off the insistence of society that noncommitment is sexy and wonderful. It can be, sometimes; that usually lasts about twenty minutes. But then there's the rest of life: desires that can't be satisfied through physical union, no matter how skilled the participants; the part of us that wants to be known beyond the sound bites we keep handy for parties, bars, and chance elevator meetings; that overwrought onion metaphor about how we're all made in layers, and it's only after a lot of peeling that you know what's inside. (Although I've always wondered about this particular image, given that the center of the onion is pretty much the same as the outside—just more onion. For a while I thought a Tootsie Pop reference would work better—remember the commercial asking, "How many licks does it take to get to the center of a Tootsie Pop?" with its suggestion that the quest for the tasty candy inside would tempt you to abandon diligence and bite through the outer shell? But then I realized that "keep licking, you're getting somewhere," wasn't quite the language we were looking for to encourage more non-sexual romantic interaction. The artichoke has possibilities—at least it has a heart—but I was still working out the finer points of that metaphor.)

Later that day, I got an e-mail advertising the newest CD from a teen singing sensation. Glancing through her song titles,

I saw this same longing: references to white knights, Romeo and Juliet, fairy tales, and long conversations where the only thing bare is your soul. I was saddened a few days later to hear that her equally famous boyfriend had dumped her for some starlet. And I wondered if she even knew that Romeo and Juliet, while a stellar example of commitment, were not exactly role models you want to pattern a life after.

Essay winner Fields ended her piece with one of those awkward stories we hate to remember: meeting a guy, hanging out a few times, ending up at his apartment for the night. Then later, asking, "when do you think we'll see each other again?" and meaning it in the most literal way possible, expecting an answer like *Monday*, or *after the holidays*... only to find yourself in the worst sort of Define The Relationship conversation, and the guy's cold assessment that there's no there, there:

"Then it came," she said. "The story. The long, boring, aggravatingly rehearsed and condescending story... He was seeing a lot of other people, and he liked me; he thought I was special. Cross my heart, he actually called me special... I tried to process it... to remember that I was actively seeking to practice some Zenlike form of nonattachment."

She used words like *casual, careless, lighthearted, fun* to describe this state she thought she was supposed to be living in, this professed nirvana everyone pursued through keeping their options open and knowing everything physically but nothing on any other level. By the time I finished reading I wanted to hug her, shake her, tell her it was worth it to expect more from life, and how anyone who survives their twenties understands how rarely *careless* ever leads to *fun*.

"Okay Jesus," I asked out loud. "Where's the hope? For

Marguerite? For my friends? For the millions of single women out there who will read this and think, 'Wow, it really is as bad as I thought'? You're the one who promised abundant life. So tell me: how do we get there?" It was one of those moments where I was quite sure he'd have no response, where my whole point in raising the subject was to point out that he'd fallen down on his promises to take care of women who need love. Then came one of those intersecting thoughts: *What is impossible with man is possible with God,* Jesus reminded me. Now, I knew this. Luke 18:27 is one of my favorite Bible passages. I have it written out on Post-its all over our house. But I still didn't know what that looked like—specifically, in here-are-your-next-steps terms—for my friends, for the essayist, for the young singer-songwriter who was just dumped in front of the whole world, for the women in their forties and fifties who e-mailed me asking if the hope I've found in Jesus might apply to them?

The word "faith" crossed my mind, along with its most famous definition. In the New Testament book of Hebrews, we're told that "Faith is being sure of what we hope for and certain of what we do not see."

Sure of what we hope for.

Suddenly, I realized that this might be the missing link for the girl who wrote the essay. She'd lost her certainty of what she hopes for, convinced by a bizarre conflagration of skewed feminism, revamped hippy jargon, and media promiscuity that she wants (or should want) something other than what she really wants.

And here, I saw room for hope.

My friend Jaime—the one who God speaks to through graffiti at Whole Foods ("and that had to be God," she says, "because they wipe down those doors every other minute")—wrote me an e-mail about the *Twilight* book series, explaining why it captivated her. I'd been mildly concerned since she spent an entire weekend holed up in her apartment reading about vampire love, but then she allayed my fears:

> You won't believe this, but the relationship that Edward and Bella have resembles the relationship that I want in someone who follows God. I imagine my perfect Christian husband to love me for me, be more amazing than I could imagine, and yet think I'm amazing, be concerned for my soul, not want to sleep with me until we're married, and get me entirely. I'm a hopeless sucker for a good love story...but it gives me hope.

I laughed at her assessment of how being a hopeless sucker gave her hope, but I understood. She got it: the vital connection between what we hope for and how we see the world, God, and the possible connections between the two. "Faith is being sure of what we hope for and certain of what we do not see." For me, this meant using whatever voice I had to suggest a well-defined hope, no matter how crazy that might look in the face of what's going on around us. Suggesting that we be honest with ourselves, and with God (He knows anyway) and trust that when He says, "Don't rush the sex," He has a method to lead us through the madness.

Chapter 16

Covered

I WAS AT A WRITING RETREAT in the small town in Maine where I grew up. As I walked the beach in between chapters, my past and present crashed about in my mind like so many colliding waves. One chilly morning, I walked out to the end of the jetty that marks the divide between ocean and river, the one built to protect the inlet from storms. An old song kept repeating in my head about how *sometimes, love just ain't enough.* I've always hated that that's true.

I can't look at the ocean and not think of God. It's just so obvious there, who's in charge. The Bible says that God drew the boundaries of the earth, telling the waves where to stop. Looking at the beach wall washed out by last year's storms, it's obvious that we don't have anywhere near that power. They say that we make plans and God laughs, and this seemed a clear illustration—God might humor our boundaries, but He's not constrained by them. The Bible also says that God draws boundaries around us—hemming us in behind and before. We can crash against them ("kicking at the goads" as one writer puts it) and even climb up over them like waves bent on destruction. I did this time and time again in search of love. I wrestled down the boundaries of my own integrity—what I'd decided I would and wouldn't do, boundaries that had held me in good stead when I was young. Other times I submitted unquestioningly to experts who redrew these boundaries, telling me that my limits were newly expanded, never explaining that this new land came at a cost. That's what I heard, out there at the end of the jetty: Jesus' warning that wise people count the cost before taking new ground. This is what I long to tell women: there's a cost to letting down our boundaries (or lying there while they're breached). It doesn't make us bad people, or take us beyond God's love. But love alone isn't enough. Our choices make us more (or less) of who we are, who we want to be. There's a cost to breaking ranks with God.

C.S. Lewis, as always, put it well when he pointed out that "what would really satisfy us would be a God who said of anything we happened to like doing, 'What does it matter so long as they are contented?' We want," he continued, "not so much a Father in Heaven as a grandfather in heaven—a senile benevolence who, as they say, 'liked to see young people enjoying themselves,' and whose plan for the universe was simply that it might truly be said at the end of each day, 'a good time was had by all'...I should very much like to live in a universe which was governed on such lines," he admitted. "But since it is abundantly clear that I don't, and since I have reason to believe, nonetheless, that God is Love, I conclude that my conception of love needs correction."

He didn't talk much about fear, not directly, but for me that's what it all came down to. Jesus describes how perfect love (his love) casts out the fear that tries to hold us down and take us captive. That kind of fear is deadly. But he also suggests a different kind of fear, a holy fear that serves us, making us unwilling to settle for anything that's not God's best.

If you consider yourself a feminist, this is the place in my story where you'll probably want to get something hard to bite down on. This is where I talk about what Steve and I discovered about men's and women's roles in the Bible — quite different from the prevailing wisdom of today — and how God designed the two to best fit together in the ever-shifting puzzle of marriage. Don't get me wrong: I'm not barefoot, and I've yet to get pregnant; I have a career and lots of big dreams, and Steve cheers me on. But it's safe to say that the structure of our marriage is unlike anything you'll come across in *Ms.* magazine or *Cosmo*.

If you've ever taken a class in women's studies, you've probably seen the word *coverture*. It's a legal term (now considered so obsolete that my spell-check is rejecting it as I type) that used to indicate that a woman had no rights, or legal existence, of her own. She was subsumed under the men in her life — first her father, then her husband. There was no need for her to vote, the thinking went, because she thought whatever her husband thought; he spoke for them both. For obvious reasons, women found this legal tradition less than charming, and ripped it down with their bare hands as soon as society allowed. I, for one, am glad. So it was with Biblical levels of fear and trembling that I waded into the spiritual concept of coverture, wondering how this ancient concept could possibly apply to

Steve and me now. I'd heard that Jesus' teachings were meant to convey good news, but it was hard for me to see how the seemingly misogynistic rantings by the Apostle Paul—filled with descriptions of women as "the weaker vessel," who should respect our husbands and "submit" to them—could be anything other than Biblically sanctioned bondage. Going in, I couldn't see where the good news was in that.

I read the passages on marriage, trying to hold my dislike of some of Paul's teachings in abeyance for long enough to get to what God might be telling me with these words. I looked at books like Shaunti Feldhahn's *For Women Only* for insight into how this might play out in this day and age, and why it might be worth it. I puzzled over (unsolicited) mail I received from groups like the left-wing National Organization for Women and the right-wing Concerned Women for America (oddly, all the latter group seemed concerned about was that the liberals might be organized) each stridently insisting on a one-size-fits-all approach to gender relations. It took me awhile to sort it out. Over time, though, what helped the most was talking to Steve. I came right out and asked him, "How do you want our marriage to work?" and then waited, cringing inside (why did I always expect him to say something horrifying?) to hear what he had to say.

"I want to help you thrive," he said. "That's my responsibility as your husband." Still, I wasn't sure what my side of this bargain looked like specifically, in day-to-day terms and if I'd like it.

Questions of gender dynamics have haunted me most of my life. I hated being left out of tryouts for freshman high school soccer because I was a girl; hated that the partners in my law firm lumped me in with other "women of childbearing age" and assumed I'd be gone in a few years; hated that a salesman at a car showroom would only talk to my boyfriend du jour when I was the one buying the car. Most of all, I hated the memory of my dad going off to work every day to have an interesting life, while Mom was (to my eyes) stuck at home raising us and cooking a never-ending array of dinners. I was so terrified of being forced into the mold of feminine subservience I thought I saw all around me that I never noticed the sexy, fun-filled agreement my parents operated within, how they'd *chosen* these roles together as a team. (You'd think I'd have caught on: whenever my sister or I did something ridiculous, Dad would tease Mom with a smile, "I thought you should go back to school to become a teacher," he'd say, "but you wanted kids...") All I saw was that it was Mom doing the dishes night after night. I rejected anything that might conscript me to that life. This was why I never learned to cook, why I didn't want to clean. Domesticity seemed like a perilous, slippery slope I could never come back from if I ever lost my footing and fell down its swift, awful slide to the housewife pit where nothing would matter beyond my ability to vacuum, apply lipstick, and whip up a good pork roast in time for dinner.

What brought me out of this funk, over time, was memoirs by widows. I'd read Madeleine L'Engle. But now I stayed up late one night to finish the tear-drenched saga of four women who had lost their husbands on September 11th. I bought Joan Didion's *The Year of Magical Thinking* in hardcover, lent it to a friend, and then bought it again in paperback. In these stories, I found the best (and worst) picture of what it looks like to thrive in the 20/20 view of their hindsight, the ones they loved gone, so they could see the spaces their husbands had filled most clearly. Here, I found words to describe the mystery of marriage: how you *are* tied in and wrapped up with your husband when you're married, no matter how determined you are to retain your independence; how there simply isn't any "me" and "you" anymore, the way there is when you're single; and how allowing oneself to be intertwined can be a gift, rather than a curse. I cried through a scene where Joan Didion's husband, John, read a passage she'd written out loud to her, exclaiming, "Dammit, don't ever tell me you can't write!" I cried because the story was beautiful, but also because Steve had just told me about a friend of ours who'd said to him, "You know you need to tell Trish to give up this writing thing, right? I mean, people don't just jot down their life story and get published." He wouldn't tell me who. But he told me how he'd countered, saying, "Actually, I think Trish *will* get published. I think her story will encourage a lot of people. I believe in her."

These moments encouraged me to exchange my independence for the hope of creating something enduring, as Didion and her husband had. And I found an odd sort of solace in the realization that if something ever happened to Steve, if I joined the ranks of the widowed, I'd know that I'd been cherished. Nothing could take that from me. This small awareness of how I'd feel if Steve died was surprisingly helpful as I sorted out how to be a good wife to him while he lived.

So Steve was my covering—what, exactly, did this mean? Coverture, for me, meant that the impact of my former bad choices wouldn't haunt me forever. I was covered by Steve's good choices, and now the beneficiary of his credit rating, his insurance coverage, and his well-timed real estate decisions. A year or so earlier, I'd read a promise in the Bible that God would "restore the years the locust had eaten," and wondered what that might look like. This, I was pretty sure, was it. I didn't deserve it, but God gave it to me anyway. I think they call that "grace."

My friend Janine married the love of her life at nineteen, and soon discovered that his type Z personality drove her type A right up a tree, where she stayed for the next five years. Before long they were in debt, in conflict, and at each other's throats. Janine discovered, like generations of women before her, that nagging made things worse, but she had no idea what else to do. She felt like she wasn't important enough to her husband for him to do the right things for them as a couple, whereas he sensed that she thought he was a screw-up, dragging her down. Secular friends told them to leave each other. Jesus-ey friends told them to pray.

A friend from the second group gave her a book suggesting that she take seriously this promise that her husband was her covering, and thank God for making this happen, rather than lamenting about how she couldn't see evidence of it yet. "Call him a mighty man of God," it suggested. "Let him make some decisions, and trust God to work things out. See what happens." Never one to dip her toe in a pool when a swan dive is possible, Janine started doing that crazy thing the Bible talks about, *calling things that are not as though they are.* She didn't make things up; she wasn't delusional or dishonest. But she prayed for Tony to make good decisions, and cheered him on when he did. When he didn't, she took her complaints to God. The results surprised them both. Not only did Tony rise to the occasion, making smart choices for them, he started lavishing her with affection and attention in a way that hadn't been true before. She wouldn't have said this was something she needed until she got it; now it's indispensable. It wasn't an instant cure-all, but gradually, this new approach changed the paradigm of their relationship, so that by the time Steve and I met them, they were one of the few couples we found who agreed with us that marriage was more *good* than *hard*. Compelling stuff, when you see it in real life.

The story of Mary and Joseph offers insight into how this works. It's a tale of almost unfathomable possibility, of God literally showing up in this couple's life—through dreams and angels (the stuff we love to read about but don't really believe happens today), guiding them to safety again and again. The most interesting thing about this story—aside from the obvious incredulity of a virgin discovering that she's pregnant and negotiating the resultant social challenges such a thing created in that time and culture—is how even though God used Mary to carry the Savior, it was Joseph He spoke to about how and where to take his family to keep them safe. Because of Joseph's willingness to believe God (who sent an angel to him in a dream, instructing him not to dismiss the pregnant Mary as he'd planned to) they avoided crises, turmoil, famine. All in all, I'd say the whole coverture thing worked out well for her.

Still, even in the midst of these great promises, I sometimes wondered if I'd be as willing to embrace this Jesus-centered wife model if I hadn't had an entire decade of experiences where I tried things out on my own terms? I've enjoyed some rare air: second and third and tenth chances most people don't get to re-create themselves. When I meet others who came to faith as adults, we seem like a less frustrated group than the lifelong Christians. It's as if the boundaries are a relief to us, a place to rest, rather than walls we've spent our lives climbing, trying to see over. It seemed like this Biblical model of wifedom came more easily to me because I'd tried everything else and experienced first-hand its limitations.

It reminded me of the Amish tradition of Rumspringa, where they set their young adults free for a year of life outside the community rules. During Rumspringa, Amish teens can wear what they want, drive cars, date, drink, whatever strikes their fancy. The point of this is so they can make a real choice about how they want to live afterwards. How terrifying a system for parents, but how wise.

I saw a reality show once where they took five Rumspringa kids and combined them with five "normal" Americans at the same point in life, then sent them on a few weeks' worth of adventures to see how they'd get along. You could see the setup, how the normals were expected to corrupt the Amish and make them see how much they'd been missing in their sheltered world. That's not how it worked out, though. The Amish teens were surprisingly aware of the costs and benefits of their choices, whereas the normals seemed drunken and miserable, oblivious to everything but their immediate wants and emotions. By the end of the show, only one of the Amish said he might not return to his community, and this wasn't because he'd found a secular girlfriend or loved to party. He wanted to go to college so he could become an engineer. It didn't go at all as producers planned — by the end even I was wondering if I could make a life with the bonnets and buggies. The show was never repeated.

I think there's something to this idea of knowing the full range of possibilities before we commit ourselves to a grown-up path. Life has texture no matter who you are. But if you have a chance to choose your challenge and pick your structure, I think that goes a long way toward helping you stick to it without feeling stuck. I'm glad I tried feminism, and being an independent woman, even though I failed. It was a little like my Rumspringa. Afterwards, I understood the boundaries—what they held in, what they kept out. And it was good to be home, and to be covered.

Chapter 17

Story

I LOVE READING memoirs. They make me think about how we tell our stories: the choices we make about what stays in and what goes, whose feelings we take into account and who we hope we won't run into again once the book goes to press. How do we make decisions we'll be happy with, a day or a week or a year down the road? It makes me think about how, even when we're not writing, we're telling other people who we are, through our words, our clothing, the things we reveal. We're all telling a story, sharing bits of ourselves. "Stories," Eugene Peterson says, "are verbal acts of hospitality."

Verbal acts of hospitality. I like that.

When I was younger—college, grad school—I struggled to find "my story." I was embarrassed to be Irish, it seemed like such an ignoble heritage. We were pale people with no queen of our own, fighting a generations-long battle over religious dogma most of us didn't even understand. We killed each other. We starved. Our native dance involved a passionless, frantic hopping, as if someone was shooting at our feet. In an era of extreme ethnic self-definition, there wasn't a whole lot there for me to craft an identity from. Back then, Bono wasn't even Bono.

I had a few other options I played on — some French lineage on my mom's side, English on my dad's. In my days of casting the widest net I could manage in the hopes of finding a husband, I even considered claiming Jewish roots to tap into their cultural treasure trove of matchmaking services (my maternal grandmother's maiden name was Silver; I hoped that might be enough to get me up over the hurdle of the whole "she looks like a map of Ireland" thing). I felt adrift in a world where friends came back from international vacations decked out in African tribal fabrics or Indian saris. They had the gentle, fierce Maya Angelou and the radical Salman Rushdie; I had Frank McCourt telling how the church leaders in his hometown hadn't cared if he had shoes or food. I soon learned that any book hailed as "A tale of Irish fortitude" was really "a story too grim to bear." Sinead O'Connor shaved her head and tore up a picture of the Pope on *Saturday Night Live*. Archie Bunker yelled at his son-in-law, Meathead, to get out of his chair. These were my people.

Then I met Steve's stepfather, Jim. Jim is Irish, too. At family gatherings it's all about laughter, just like the family I grew up in. Talking to Jim made me realize what it means for me to be Irish: it's not native dress or dance or a side in some religious conflict. I'm Irish because of my humor.

Growing up in our house, the valued skill was not grades or sports, but finding the absurd in the mundane events of everyday life. At dinner each night, we told tales of the dumbest thing we'd done that day. But not in a way that put ourselves down. The challenge was to make it funny—to make other people feel at ease, rather than uncomfortable, despite the fact that we'd just shared things most folks would deny. My parents excelled at this, and encouraged this gift in their children. This is why, after putting our house up as collateral for an imprisoned family member's bail, Dad hung an American flag at the end of our driveway with a sign that said, "Freedom Road." This is why Mom still tells the story of the day she went to the bank in her slippers, with her polyester pants on backwards. My sister, Meg, once used a tennis racket to hit the ball for our fetch-loving Golden Retriever. Never the most athletic member of our clan (again—who is when you're Irish? Doesn't the phrase "Irish Olympic Team" sound like the setup for a *Saturday Night Live*/Sinead O'Connor reunion skit?), she pelted the ball directly at the dog's snout and sent poor Dusty scurrying under the deck for cover. We lived for these moments. Where other folks (the ones decked out in the tribal fabrics or saris, perhaps) might be embarrassed by such misadventures, they were gold for us—guaranteed laugh generators to draw us together, get us through difficult times, and remind us that while perspective might not be everything, it counts for a lot.

I think a lot about creativity: where it comes from, how we capture it, the difference between the story in our head and the one we wrestle with, trying to create. I've tried all sorts of creative tools, both in my life and in my writing: gratitude journals, *The Artist's Way*, *Drawing on the Right Side of the Brain*, even an internet group where everyone writes a novel in a single month. I guess I'm not that structured, because these plans rarely hold my attention. To be honest, my "plan" for creativity is that when I have a chance to try something interesting, I give it a shot. And when I think of something interesting, I stop what I'm doing and write it down. Simple stuff, admittedly. But over time it adds up.

Despite my lack of a system, I love hearing what works for other people, what goes into creating a creative life. I heard a great tidbit of advice in a talk by *Eat, Pray, Love* author Elizabeth Gilbert. I admire her as much as any other memoirist I know — her metaphors make me cry with envy — and we have some odd things in common: She wrote a book about lobstermen in Maine; my Dad was a lobsterman in Maine. She grew up in the same Connecticut town where I hid after my bad marriage. We both wrote books about spiritual searching after the first life we'd built fell apart. (And my publisher blatantly copied her book cover for the paperback of mine.) So in many ways, it feels like we're connected. Not sisters, perhaps, but maybe second cousins. Anyway...she was talking about the unexpected turn her life has taken: how at the age of forty, she might have as many as four decades of writing life ahead of her, but it's entirely probable that her greatest success has already happened. "Suddenly," she said, "I understand why so many writers drink gin at nine in the morning." In the way only a secure bestselling author can, she boldly offered a rather woo-woo spiritual perspective to her analytical audience, describing how the ancient Greeks and Romans understood that creativity came from outside of us, rather than within. The Greeks had *daemons*, the Romans had *geniuses*. Creative types depended on various fairies who lived in the walls that could be coaxed out from time to time to bring inspiration. This, she claimed, helped keep artists sane. (At which point I had to applaud her courage: only someone with her record of book sales could claim with a straight face that an awareness of fairies hiding in the walls helps creative types *maintain* their sanity...) But I saw her point. If things went well, she explained, they couldn't take credit; if they bombed, it wasn't their fault. She advocated a return to this system, and said her approach now is a three-part mantra: *Don't be afraid. Don't be daunted. Do your job.*

I'm less inclined than she to trust every random spirit that wanders by trying to get my attention, but I think she's onto something with this idea that it's not just about us. In fact, her words sound strikingly similar to what God said to heroes like Moses, Joshua, Gideon, and Mary...pretty much everyone in the Bible He called to do something important received similar marching orders: *Do not be afraid. Be bold and very courageous.* We show up for our lives, but in a way, that's the only thing we can take credit for. The things that matter most—love, friendship, marriage, children, art, the legacy we leave when our days on earth are done—are largely up to God. Great stories happen when we're there to live them: on the job, undaunted, unafraid. That, I think, is a pretty good strategy.

I watched a reality show called *Ruby*. The star of the show, Ruby, once weighed over five hundred pounds, but she was working hard to lose the weight, and letting the world watch. She'd lost about a hundred pounds, and on almost every episode, she'd say to one of her friends, "Thank you for helping me make my dreams come true." Her dreams were simple things: camping out under the stars, taking a plane across the country to see a friend's new baby. But they were happening because she had the courage to want them. In other words, we have to *have* dreams for them to come true. It made me wonder if I were in a room full of people and asked, "When was the last time you saw a dream of yours come true?" what the response would be. Would there be waving hands and encouraging stories, or silence?

There's not much to encourage real dreaming once we're adult. I remember feeling an abrupt shift after law school—until that point, I'd had my whole life mapped out in two, three, and four year increments: get into college, get through each semester, pass the LSAT, get into law school, make *Law Review*, get through each year, find a job, pass the bar exam...And then suddenly there I was in my cute suit, sitting in my office with my name on a plaque outside the door, new business cards in the shiny holder someone gave me as a graduation gift (along with a funny note saying it was about time I got to work), and nothing to shoot for other than partnership, six or seven years away. Worst of all, I didn't even understand how you made partner, other than bringing in new clients, and I wasn't sure where or how I was supposed to meet the decision makers of major corporations and convince them to shift their legal work to me.

Without a goal, I floundered. That first year, I made due with billed hours, shooting to be in the top ten among associates each month. For the most part, I succeeded, but that was more because I was prone to daydream during each task than because I was in any way productive. But my depression at the end of the year—when my accumulated hours went back to zero along with everybody else at the firm and I needed to start over—was so discouraging that I lost the will to bill. I even lost the will to daydream.

Where do we find dreams? I wonder if, like Ruby, we need to look at what seems impossible. Here's the catch, though: it has to require some effort on our part, to be something we can work toward. Work gives life; it creates momentum. It gets us out of bed in the morning/to the gym/in front of the laptop. Without a dream, it's tough to do the work. But without the work, it's not much of a dream.

I once read an article by a self-help guru who said that the best way to negotiate life was to think of yourself as a leaf floating along on a swiftly moving river. If we just go with the flow, she suggested, floating rather than fighting, the current will take us to where we're supposed to be. I couldn't help thinking, *But if the leaf is floating down the river, doesn't that mean it's dead?* That didn't seem like much of a model for life. I've flailed about in a whole host of rivers. I've tried to float. Every time, the current swept me past the shore I was aiming for, to places that were, let's be honest, kind of horrific. Floating is not the answer. At a certain point efforts—often in the form of hard work, internal struggle, and tough decisions that might not be my first choice—are required when I have a specific destination in mind.

Here in the Northeast, I don't meet many folks who long to float aimlessly along the river of life to see where it takes them. That's not the tenor of our region. If we're going to trek down a river, we plan ahead: a submersible raft, a top-of-the-line paddle made of some complex polymer invented by a millionaire MIT dropout, and a full North Face outfit to make sure we look the part. We'll have a plan, hire a guide, plug the trip into some iPhone app to set goals for how far to paddle each day and which important scenic things to take in. The general vibe is that we're going somewhere — quickly — and there's no time to waste. So we'll listen to pretty much anyone who promises to shave a few minutes off our travel time, ever aware that our best effort is no guarantee.

Hope is ancillary here. A slightly reviled fallback position for those whose first fifteen attempts to make their life plan work fail. Some of us have failed spectacularly, gathering enough bang for our blown buck to generate material for an "aren't you glad you're not me?" memoir. (*He Loves Me, He Loves Me Not* — available at finer booksellers near you.) Others simply give up and putter along, assuming some sort of life will accumulate along the way. But that rarely works.

President Obama talked about *The Audacity of Hope* in his second book. Regardless of your thoughts on his politics or presidency, it's a fabulous title. It makes me think of how often my audacity has been hopeless — not based in anything that could deliver the results. In the Psalms — which are really just prayers of people who put their need in writing — there are repeated encouragements to put our hope in God, like a bank deposit. It's as if each morning we do a drive-through and drop off whatever hope we have with Him, so it can collect interest or multiply somehow in a way that wouldn't happen if we carried it around all day. Other Psalms say that our hope comes *from* God — that it's like a loop where He gives us hope, almost to see what we do with it. Will we charge off on our own like a kid with a fistful of allowance money barreling toward the candy store, or will we bring it back to Him? Will we come back? Will we trust? Will we believe? Will we invest? These seem like the questions of faith we spend our lives working out.

I once had a dream (the nighttime kind) where I was surfing this huge wave. It was one of those half-awake dreams where I sensed something bigger was going on, like God was talking to me about something that was going to happen in the future. *Keep your focus and you'll be fine,* He seemed to say. *But if you freak out or panic, you'll wipe out.* I woke up but couldn't stop thinking about it. My knowledge of surfing was limited to a three-part special episode of *The Brady Bunch* where Greg was taken out by a wave when he was wearing the evil tiki idol as a necklace. But I kept seeing my feet on that surfboard (which has never happened in real life but was surprisingly easy to imagine), and realizing how small that board is. Those are some pretty tight boundaries: step off and you're done. It felt like God was telling me that I didn't have to take on all the things I might be tempted to try. There were boundaries to what he'd created me to create, and to focus on—specific things that would give me that experience of riding the giant wave rather than wiping out. I didn't have to float helplessly down the river. But I had to keep my feet on the board. I've been trying to figure out exactly what that means ever since.

Chapter 18

Heroes, Hope, and Rescue

MY FRIEND CHRISTOPHER, A gifted composer, came back from a three-month sabbatical filled with ideas and inspiration, not the least of which was a multimedia celebration of the arts exploring the theme of "Rescue." He asked if he could use one of the chapters from my first book to create a comedic monologue. I said yes immediately, thinking of how funny it would be to see some of my quirkier antics played out by an actress onstage. "Which part did you have in mind?" I asked.

"Chapter seven," he said. I wasn't sure how to reply. Chapter seven was the least comedic chapter in the book. It was where I describe—in painful detail that had prompted hours of careful parsing in the office of my publisher's attorney—the emotional abuse in my first marriage. It was filled with fights and insults, dangerous situations, and my mother's heroic attempt to help me leave. It revealed how until the violence escalated, I'd been too stubborn to bet on myself to start over. "There are some good moments there,"

Christopher said when I expressed my doubt. "Trust me."

He offered to let me act the part myself, but I declined. I couldn't imagine re-creating the worst scenes of my life in front of an audience. And I hadn't acted since the seventh grade — how embarrassing would it be if I couldn't remember my own lines? Instead, Christopher cast an actress named Barbara. It was a poignant choice; unbeknownst to either of them, one of Barbara's monologues, offered as a sermon illustration at our church seven years earlier, had helped me hold on to my fledgling hope that Jesus might have the answers I was searching for. I remembered vividly hearing her speak Lily Tomlin's classic words as she described the longing inside of us: "I always wanted to be somebody, but now I realize I should have been more specific."

To promote the show, Christopher's team created a film profiling the artists — painters, musicians, cooks, dancers, actresses, writers. Christopher asked us each to speak for a few moments, reflecting on how the theme of rescue played out in our creative endeavors. In a way, almost everything I'd written — my book, blog posts, e-mails to people I loved — came back to a few related ideas: our need to be rescued, the hope of unseen possibilities, the challenge of expecting miracles. I've always been grateful that in the Biblical accounts of Jesus' life, his death on the cross is not the drawn-out, vividly gruesome affair we've since made it out to be. It was horrific, but that's only part of the story. The bigger theme is heroic victory — how Jesus came back to life, saving us from evils we were plagued by (and those we had yet to imagine). I didn't mention this in the taping, but it was in the back of my mind. *How can I not write about rescue?* I thought. *It's the best part of the story.*

⁓᠀⁓

You may have read this on my website, on the page called My Story:

> My dream, ever since I was a little girl, was to be a super-hero. Specifically, I wanted to be one of the Wonder Twins, meeting with Superman and Wonder Woman at the Hall of Justice on Saturday mornings to fight evil and save the world. Lacking a twin, I got a law degree instead, thinking it would give me evil-fighting superhero powers. As it turns out, I was wrong.
>
> Shortly after realizing that I hated billable hours, I ended (read: fled) my career in law, and spent the next few years trying to make sense of the world. I couldn't shake the belief that life could/should/would be different—better, somehow—if only I could figure out what really mattered. I wanted to know how things like spirituality and luck and intuition worked, and how I could make them work for me. So I embarked on a quest to find the right God, but spent much of my time trying to find the right guy. At a certain point, after accumulating a heaping pile of mistakes on both counts, I came to see that the two might be intertwined.
>
> The good news is, after much trial and error, I finally found them both: the God, and the guy. Now I live in Cambridge, Massachusetts, with my superhero-husband Steve, and our genetically improbable mixed-breed dog.

And while I sit at my laptop typing each day, the Wonder Twin dream lives on...

You probably thought I was kidding. I wasn't. Ever since I was a little girl, I was certain, in that determined-little-girl kind of way, that I was going to do something BIG with my life. Now granted, at that point, I thought this meant that I would become a baton-twirling superstar. But as that dream lost its luster, I looked around and saw a startling truth: the best example of the kind of life I wanted was what I saw on Saturday morning, when the Super Friends got together. They had great jobs, a sense of purpose and accomplishment, they made the world a better place—what's not to love? And (perhaps most importantly) they had each other. Their powers worked together to conquer evil and save the day. Who doesn't want to be part of a winning team?

I have this sense that we all long to be part of something big. Deep inside, I think we all want to be superheroes. I think our cultural devouring of *Harry Potter* means something, as does our enduring love of all things *Star Wars* (prequels notwithstanding), the feeling I got in my gut as I watched *The Matrix*, and the phenomenal success of a certain three-part epic filmed in New Zealand. What if these books and movies affect us the way they do because they tap into something we know is real— the battle between good and evil, light and dark, hope and despair? What if the possibility of miracles in our everyday lives harkens back to some of our most beloved childhood games, when we wondered (and half-believed), *What if it's true?* This is, in essence, what I want to ask people: What if it's true? What could this mean for you? For us? For the world?

Part of the reason I was excited to have my story portrayed on stage was the chance to support the two real-life superhero organizations the event would benefit: Love146 and Rebuild Africa. I wanted to be part of their stories.

Love146 is comprised of a group of people dedicated to ending child sex slavery and exploitation. The name comes from an experience founder Rob Morris had when he went into a brothel in Southeast Asia with investigators, posing as a customer. The little girls he saw—some as young as four or five—didn't even have names, just numbers customers used to order the child they wanted. Most of the girls had glazed expressions, already inured to the grim reality of their plight. But as he looked into the room where the children were held, he saw one girl look out. There was still fight in her eyes. He was captivated by that tiny ray of hope. Her number was 146.

Today, Love146 builds safehomes in countries where children are most at risk, working with prevention, aftercare, and reintegration. Their promotional video offers this compelling call to action: *Love protects. Love restores. Love defends. Love empowers.*

Responding to this call, my friend Pascha traveled to Thailand, Cambodia, and the Philippines to see Love146's work firsthand. She came home awed, overwhelmed, and determined to help. She and her husband, Paul, started a chapter of Love146 here in Boston, and her experiences on that trip—witnessing firsthand lives saved and true heroic rescue—changed her perspective on what God can do through us if we're willing to be part of a larger story.

Rebuild Africa was created by a member of our church, Bill Massaquoi, who returned to his native Liberia with a plan of restoration after studying here in Cambridge. His dream is to heal his country from the ravages of civil war by releasing local potential. Rebuilding has started on a small scale, in a village of approximately 950 people called Fassavolu. They've built a kiln to fire bricks, trained workers on how to construct frames and joists, implemented programs to encourage education, and hosted a leadership conference to inspire hope. He's helping his people start over, one brick at a time.

As I learned more about these organizations, the level of human need was overwhelming. I felt impotent and small, certain in a new way that no matter what I did in my lifetime to shore up the endless waves of longing, it would never be enough. But at the same time, I was equally certain of this: Our efforts have momentum and power, and there's a larger plan for how we can make a difference. The superhero dream is possible.

Two weeks before the Artist's Event launched, Steve and I embarked on what we thought was an exciting new chapter of our dream. We moved to Central New York to join the pastoral team of another Vineyard Church. Steve would be the Pastor of Connections; I'd preach on occasional Sunday mornings. The church was smaller than ours, and we hoped to use our skills to add to what was already happening there, to help the people of that area grow and thrive. With the blessing of our friends and family here in Cambridge, we set out on this new adventure.

It turned out to be a disaster the likes of which we never could have imagined.

To couch the story in euphemism: We walked into a building that looked fine from a distance. But once we were inside, it was hard not to notice that the roof was, well ... *on fire.* We mentioned this to our new colleagues, with observations like,

"You seem to be choking on this smoke" and "Do you realize that the whole place could collapse at any moment?"

We thought that maybe we could help—put out the fire, prevent casualties, rebuild. But that's not how it played out. "The fire is no big deal," everyone insisted. "We've lived with it this long—why put it out now?"

You can't rescue anyone who doesn't want to be saved.

In the aftermath—as the fire was turned up and directed straight at us—we found ourselves praying for our own rescue, calling on friends from home to help extricate us from the mess. My sister flew from Maine to help pack our apartment. Steve's mother lent money for a truck, and a lifelong friend of Steve's rented us an apartment back in Cambridge even though we had no idea when or where either of us would find new jobs. There was no time to cry or breathe or process. All we could do was get out.

As we left that town for the last time—Steve in the rented truck, me following behind in our car—I cranked up the CD that had been like an anthem to us that summer, reminding me that life was bigger than the circumstances in front of us. It was called *The World Awaits,* by Ryanhood. The duo sang about keeping hope alive in the wake of disappointment, and I found myself belting out the first song as loud as I could as if to shake off the evil shroud of smoke we'd been covered in.

Ready to go?
Honey let's begin
And try to see by the light of the sun and tell it like it is.
I wanna sing so deep
Laugh so long
Even the silence himself wants to sing and laugh along.

When we arrived in Cambridge eight hours later, we were met by a team of friends from our home church who welcomed us back and schlepped all of our belongings—the same boxes and furniture some of them had moved just four months before—up three more flights of stairs. As I told a friend later, the only thing that kept me from bursting into grateful tears was the knowledge that nothing makes men more uncomfortable than the spectacle of a sobbing female. So I held it in, pointing silently to different rooms as they cheerfully brought up load after load. My stoicism was all I had left in me that day to express my gratitude.

As we sorted out this new/old life, I received an e-mail with a link to the video of the staged scene from my book. Steve and I curled up on the couch, the laptop between us, and hit play.

The stage was black, and then Barbara came forward into a dim light. It was bleak, yet powerful. As she spoke my words, describing all the fear and horror, tears rolled like raindrops down my face. It wasn't the memories she evoked, although as she described that last day, when my then-husband threw a giant jar of change at me, it transported me right back to the spot where I'd stood between the living room and kitchen. I could feel the scratch of the rug on my knees as I gathered up the quarters. I could hear Janet Jackson singing in the background about her own abusive husband. But that wasn't what brought me to tears. What astonished me was how far that story had traveled, and how it had been transformed. Seven years later, it had been published in a memoir that was in bookstores around the world, now a small moment in a larger story, not about abuse, but rather the victory of true love. It was performed on a stage to highlight the idea that rescue is possible, to raise money and awareness for two organizations working to bring happily ever after to some of the most hopeless places on earth. The Bible promised that God would use the hard parts of my past for good, that nothing would be wasted. In my wildest dreams, I'd never imagined it could go this far. It gave me hope that this new part of our story — the disappointment and betrayal, the rescue — wouldn't be lost either, that God would redeem it, and use it to reach out a hand of rescue to others who don't want to stay in a burning building, no matter how safe everyone around them says it is. And the words I spoke that day in the video are true now more than ever:

> *I have this idea that we all have inside of us this hope. So you have reality and things have turned out a certain way and some of that's been good and some of that's been disappointing. But then you also have these dreams inside of what could be, and it feels like there's this huge gap between them. I feel like my work is all about saying, "Don't settle — the rescue is coming. It's coming for you. It's coming for you in a way that will feel personal and will take you to your other side, whatever that might be."*

Rescue. It's coming.

Chapter 19

Four Words

MY FRIEND LIZ got married last weekend to a great guy. He was in love with her for a couple of years before she caught up with him, but watching them leaning in toward each other up there at the altar (looking for all the world like they might grab their rings and make a run for the honeymoon suite before the hymns and the vows were finished) made it pretty clear that she had, indeed, caught up.

Our friend Chelsea performed the ceremony, and gave one of the most poignant and practical wedding charges I'd ever heard. Recognizing that Liz and Hiromu were unlikely to remember the details of their ceremony, Chelsea distilled her wisdom down into four words, two for each of them.

Liz's words were PRAYER WORKS. Chelsea pointed out that one of the scriptures in their ceremony was from the seventeenth chapter of Jeremiah, which talks about how people are blessed who put their confidence in God, how they are like a tree, planted by water, with deep roots. She talked about overcoming the first response of fear with a second response of prayer. "Here are some of the implications of prayer working," she said. "It means that God cares about all those little details that you care about; that God is powerful enough to make actual changes in your life; that God honors your earnestness; and that God desires to remain connected to you at all times. Liz, prayer actually works," she concluded. "It will be the conduit for the things you want with Hiromu."

Hiromu's two words were LOVE WINS. Chelsea talked about how he'd suffered, waiting for Liz to fall in love with him, and how he was right to keep loving her. "Love is," she said, "an excellent strategy. One of your tasks as a husband will be to take great, deep confidence in your love for Liz. Romance and passion and being extremely cute together are not just the end goals you are dreaming of. They are in fact your method of getting there."

Prayer works. Love wins. If I hadn't just spent two years trying to write about what it means to believe in happily ever after, I'd have posted those words on our refrigerator and worked on a novel instead. Because that about sums it up. Not just for marriage, but for life.

In the weeks that followed Liz and Hiromu's wedding, many of us who were there had our own opportunities to put that charge to the test, as life got very real in a wide array of ways that left us all with more questions than answers. We prayed, and we loved, and we waited to see what God would do. In many ways, we're still waiting. But there are hints, and glimpses of bigger hope at play, signs that we're not fools to believe Paul's promise to the Romans that God uses all things for the good of those who love Him, who are called according to His purpose. And as you'd expect in a maze, the path continues to twist and turn and double back on itself so rapidly that if I didn't take the time to look up and recalibrate, I'd have no idea where I was.

My friend Amy Julia is living in a similar tension between the now and the not yet, as she and her husband watch their daughter Penny, born four years ago with Down syndrome, grow. "Peter and I watched the movie *I Am Sam* last week," she e-mailed me. "It's the story of a mentally disabled adult, Sam, with a seven-year-old daughter. According to the movie, Sam has the 'mental capacity of a seven-year-old.' The state takes Lucy, his daughter, away, and the movie traces their relationship and the courtroom drama that ensues. I cried the whole way through, and Peter wasn't exactly stoic about it either. Afterwards, as we talked about the film, I said, 'Down syndrome doesn't mean anything right now. Or it doesn't mean anything that really impacts our lives. It means that Penny can't jump. It means that she's short. It means we go to the eye doctor and she wears glasses. But it doesn't impact her relationships, so it doesn't really mean anything right now.' That movie reminded me that one day it will mean something. And I have to trust that as much as will be taken from her will be given back to her. We have to trust. Who knows when that will happen, or what the real significance of Penny's extra chromosome will be for her or for us? I suppose the thing to do at the moment is be grateful."

I agreed—that's the thing to do. This is how I'm trying to live now, the best answer I've found for the questions of faith and life: Prayer works. Love wins. Notice. Be grateful. This is the story Steve and I are building, on Jesus' promise for our lives. If his death and resurrection conquered sin and restored our relationship with God, this means that if we choose to, we get a glimpse of the life Adam and Eve had in the Garden of Eden, back before the snake and the fruit.

Naked, Unashamed.

A real honeymoon — happily ever after.

Not just me, but any of us.

A maze of grace.

Amazing Grace.

Amen.

Acknowledgments

ONE OF MY FAVORITE parts of being a writer is having a chance to thank people—I feel abundantly blessed.

Thank you Elisabeth Weed, my superhero agent, for believing in me and making the impossible possible. Thank you to the team at Hachette: Michelle Rapkin, Rolf Zettersten, Harry Helm, Jana Burson, Veronica Sepe, Shanon Stowe, Valerie Russo, and everyone who has contributed to taking my pages from Word doc to bound books. Thanks also to Chris Park and Sarah Sper McLellan, who cheered me up and on throughout this process.

Speaking of cheering me on, thank you to my family. You're the ones who planted this crazy idea in my head that marriage can be good. Mom and Dad: thanks for showing me how love and laughter sweeten life, and for being such amazing parents. Meg and Patrick Raymond: thank you for all the votes of confidence, the thirty-six-hour emergency rescue mission, high times on Lake Mooselookmeguntic, and the warm security of sisterhood. It's nice to know I'll always have someone to boogie with to disco music at Target. Owen and Lily: thanks for being so incredibly cool, fun, and awesome. Here's to team U-day! Thanks to my brothers, Chris and Eric, for proving through your own stories that happily ever after is worth fighting for. And thank you to my in-laws: Mom and Dad Conway, Lisa, and Jimmy, for being so gracious when Steve's new wife published a book about what a mess she used to be. I love being part of your family.

To Dave and Grace Schmelzer, Senior Pastors of The Vineyard Christian Fellowship of Greater Boston: Thank you for being such loving friends, fun encouragers, wise role models, and great leaders. We're grateful for all you've invested in us, and the myriad ways you've helped as we've negotiated perilous terrain.

And to our amazing church family: Chris and Aimee Radom, Dominic and Kristina Kaiser, Dan and Julia Maranan, Paul and Pascha Griffiths, Chuck and Marianne Snekvik, Andrew and Val Snekvik, Brian Housman, Gwen Bruno, Hiromu and Liz Boschee Nagahara, Laurie Bittman, Tim and Jess Vaverchek, Alex and Erica Charis, John Robinson, Danny and Deidre Tao, Christopher and Dorothy Greco, Ivy Anthony, Stephanie Acker, Esther Cho, Jaime Babstock, Carrie Working, Liane Young, Jonathan and JulieAnna Facelli, and Alexis Kruza. Thank you for showing us what grace looks like in real time.

To our extended family: Gavin and Emily Long, the Genzyme Friday Group, Abby and Ryan Green, Cameron Hood, Eric and Quinn Chapman, Amy Julia Becker, Lynette Estes, Kristen Fincken Mahan, Mark and Kathy DeHaan, and Lisa Robertson. Steve and I are grateful for your support and love.

To my fellow writers and bloggers: A.J. Jacobs, Cathleen Falsani, Gretchen Rubin, Sarah Dunn, Kathleen Norris, Heather King, Lisa Patton, Allison Winn Scotch, Laura Dave, Shaunti Feldhahn, Nancy French, Kristin Armstrong, Alison

Pace, Anne Lamott, Donald Miller, Patricia Wood, Amy MacKinnon, Holly Kennedy, John Elder Robison, Trish Garner, Stephanie Elliott, Stacy Brazalovich, Sara None, and Larramie...thank you for the motivation, inspiration, and for creating such an awesome community of creative people. It's an honor to "know" you all.

Special thanks to Paul Griffiths for jumping in to help at the last minute (and writing the funniest line in this book), to George Plante for giving us shelter, and to Ryanhood (aka Ryan Green and Cameron Hood) for writing the soundtrack to this season of my life.

And finally (always): Thank you Steve, my amazing husband, for living these moments with me and for being such an awesome partner in this adventure. Thank you Jesus, for exceeding our expectations, making sure we're never bored, and helping us find our way through your Maze of Grace.